VOLUME 3

Index It RIGHT!

Advice From the Experts

Edited by
ENID L. ZAFRAN

AMERICAN
SOCIETY FOR
INDEXING

First Printing, 2014

Index It Right! Advice From the Experts, Volume 3

ISBN 978-1-57387-500-4

Published by
Information Today, Inc.
143 Old Marlton Pike
Medford, NJ 08055

in association with

American Society for Indexing, Inc.
1628 E. Southern Ave., #9-223
Tempe, AZ 85282

Printed in the United States of America

President and CEO: Thomas H. Hogan, Sr.
Editor-in-Chief and Publisher: John B. Bryans
VP Graphics and Production: M. Heide Dengler
Managing Editor: Amy M. Reeve
Book Designer: Kara Mia Jalkowski
Cover Designer: Lisa Conroy
ASI Publications Chair: Enid L. Zafran
Indexer: Eve Morey Christiansen

Contents

iii

Introduction

Enid L. Zafran © 2014

"Index It Right!" started in 2005 as a series I conceived to give expert advice on a wide variety of indexing topics and specialties. Unlike the "Indexing Specialties" series where each publication is devoted to a particular type of indexing (e.g., legal, medical, cookbooks), "Index It Right!" volumes are like a smorgasbord of tasty dishes. It has been especially rewarding to see how enthusiastically they have been greeted by the indexing and information community.

Volume 3 concludes my time as the publications chair for the American Society for Indexing (ASI). I have held this post since 1998 and during that time have worked with Information Today, Inc. (ITI) to produce almost 20 books devoted to the field of indexing. Every single contribution was written by a volunteer who understood the need to expand the literature available about indexing and to take a practical, hands-on approach. These works were never intended for "ivory tower" reflection but to guide indexers in applying their art.

I want to acknowledge the assistance of Rebecca McCorkle, who generously proofread the submissions for this volume. And in general, I want to express my gratitude to John Bryans, editor-in-chief of the ITI books division, who has always offered the best advice, remained supportive even in recessionary times, and saw the usefulness of our endeavors. Amy Reeve, managing editor of the books division, has shepherded the titles through production, and her attention to detail has impressed me with every book on which we have collaborated.

For this specific volume, I have been lucky to work with some longtime associates once again: Frances Lennie, who writes about indexing as an "art form," Fred Leise, who has blazed the path for indexers to become taxonomists, and Martin White, who has the most impressive resumé and a long career as an indexer of scholarly books. This book shows how the field of indexing has evolved in the past decade to be more than just words on a paper page. In addition to Fred Leise's chapter on ecommerce taxonomies, Chuck Knapp discusses how his world as an indexing manager changed when he moved into taxonomy creation at Bloomberg BNA. Glenda Browne and Mary Coe both have played instrumental roles in the development of an indexing standard for ebooks. Their article offers insight into how indexes work within that electronic environment and the importance of gaining industry acceptance to provide the best functionality possible.

Covering specific niches of indexing has always been one of the hallmarks of "Index It Right!" and so this volume adds to the growing list: history (Connie Binder), multicultural texts (Celeste Newbrough), and medical and science (Anne-Marie Downey). For all the mathematics-phobes out there, Cynthia Landeen shows how math can be approached with the same analysis as any other field of indexing.

At the ASI Conference in San Diego in 2012, I met Lai Heung Lam when she presented her talk "Understanding Chinese, Japanese, and Korean Personal Names" and asked her immediately to contribute to this volume. Her explanation of how to deal with Romanized Chinese names and the various transliteration systems will prove helpful to indexers and editors. This topic was touched upon in *Indexing Names* (edited by Noeline Bridge, ASI/ITI, 2012); Lai Lam's article augments that volume.

To help in the mechanics of indexing and improve productivity and accuracy, Scott Smiley has devised useful tips for the use of patterns. These powerful shortcuts prove why indexing software exceeds the capabilities of word-processing software—once you use patterns, you will definitely be hooked.

Lucie Haskins has served the indexing profession in many capacities, and for this book she describes her teaching role with the Berkeley course for beginner indexers. For those who are considering adding "teaching" to their skills, Lucie will offer an insightful view into the work involved as well as the satisfaction to be obtained.

And this volume has one of the most complete treatments of journal indexing I have seen. For that I thank Linda Dunn, who has taught this indexing specialty as well as worked in it for many years. She has produced an article that will become a major reference for any indexer working with serial publications. She also describes the experience of using a thesaurus to assign terms.

As in other volumes, ASI is pleased to give a newer indexer the opportunity to create the index to this book. Eve Morey Christiansen is still in the early years of what I hope will become a long and successful career for her.

I appreciate the opportunity that ASI has afforded me to create these publications and fulfill my desire to educate others about indexing. While I have often heard people describe what I do as "the most tedious thing they have ever heard," the very opposite is true: Indexing has provided me with minutes, hours, days, months, and years of amusement and education. And I have tried to share that with you, the readers of these books.

Chapter 1

Indexing as Canvas, Musings On

Frances S. Lennie © 2014

I've always had a thing for paintings. I enjoy viewing them, thinking about the artistic approach, appreciating the artist's technique, and relating to the subject matter. In many ways indexes and indexing provide not dissimilar diversions—except our medium is words not visual images.

PORTRAITURE

I first started thinking about indexes akin to pieces of art during an interview for *Key Words*[1] quite some time ago. In that piece, I compared indexes to the commissioning of portraits, in that the indexer (artist) does not know if the expectations or preferences of the author/editor (sitter) have been met until the completed index (canvas) has been delivered and viewed. I also mused that perhaps one is hired because of one's personal indexing style, just as particular artists may be commissioned[2] for their known handling of portrait subjects.

With a few remarkable exceptions (Pablo Picasso in his Cubist period comes to mind), one could expect most portraits to contain a number of standard elements such as facial features and hair. Facial expressions, adornment, and context, however, may be rendered differently. If you look at the many images of Queen Elizabeth II, you will immediately recognize the person, even over the course of her lengthy reign, but each with different accoutrements and expressiveness.[3] Indexers speak of the 60/40 rule: The same text indexed by different experienced indexers will produce indexes with strong commonalities (60 percent) and items differing (40 percent) in perceived importance or audience interest. I like to think that, in this regard, indexes are like portraits. Except that, of course, rarely is the same identical text ever indexed by more than one indexer (only perhaps if the initial result was not agreeable to the author or editor). A close approximation would be the indexing of a new edition: same author, same topic, but with some changes in content, and a different indexer. However, unless the clients disliked the earlier index, they usually insist that the overall style, organization, and length remain the same.

IMPRESSIONISM VS. PRECISIONISM

Portraiture is a particular form of artistic endeavor, just as book indexing is one form of indexing. The art categories of Impressionism and Precisionism are broadly commensurate to the depth of indexing and the related indexing concepts of specificity (exhaustiveness) and retrieval (recall).[4]

With broad brush strokes, an impressionist artist can convey a sense of place, mood, or object. With great attention to detail, a precisionist artist depicts the place or object exactly as it appears, leaving little to the imagination or sensibility of the viewer.

An indexer may similarly outline the scope of a text with broad topic and concept headings providing little specificity for the user but probably resulting in a high rate of retrieval which requires further scrutiny. The converse of this is the indexer who indexes exhaustively, providing the user with a very high degree of detail resulting in limited but highly relevant retrieval.

Because indexers work with words, not images, we have the luxury of mixing the two artistic opposites to great effect. We help guide the user with an overview of the metatopic (an impression of the scope of the text) interleaved with whatever level of detail (precision) the text requires. We can also combine (mash up) multiple indexes into a cohesive and workable whole. Can you imagine the artistic outcome of Claude Monet's impressionist *Waterloo Bridge* (magart.rochester.edu/ Obj4132) integrated with Ralston Crawford's precisionist *Whitestone Bridge* (mag.rochester.edu/seeingAmerica/pdfs/60.pdf)? Indexers can do this because, unlike the art viewer who is able to view and appreciate the whole image at once, the index user (as far as I'm aware) concentrates on individual terms in separate excursions into the index. With the advent of ebooks, this may change as the ability to access and view multiple terms simultaneously becomes a possibility. A new indexing art form to be sure!

THE ARTIST AT WORK

I've never had the privilege of observing an artist at work other than on video (Jackson Pollock comes to mind). I have read accounts of how Monet would have several different canvases in progress and available at the same time (the better to catch the subject of the painting—river, haystacks, facade of Rouen cathedral—in different light), and I saw Johannes Vermeer's methods depicted in the movie *Girl With a Pearl Earring* (adapted from the book of the same name by Tracy Chevalier).

I have, however, heard colleagues describe how they work, which is probably as varied as the different techniques employed by artists, with no single one better than any other *as long as* the result admirably serves its intended purpose. Indexers face challenges similar to those of artists: arrangement and organization (composition);

choice of wording (color and brushstrokes); and, if we think about the 60/40 rule just discussed, how much background information should be added after the primary subject (metatopic) has been fully addressed. Here, the artist possibly has greater license, but the background still has to be compatible with the primary subject and understandable by the intended audience. For example, Renaissance paintings of religious subject matter included visually coded political, social, or religious references in foreground or background. Perhaps a visual cross-reference to matters of related interest?

Artists and indexers also approach their work in similar ways. An artist may produce an initial sketch or study; an indexer may draft an outline or concept map of major terms or topics. I confess that I do neither but tend to "word-doodle" through the first chapter or so until I find the rhythm and cadence of the text. In artistic terms, one might think of this as my "Jackson Pollack" approach—scattered but hopefully less messy.

An artist's editing tools are his brush and paint to best render his subject; ours are the words we use to convey contextual accuracy. Words can be dry, challenging, and frustratingly elusive, but when you strike just the right note, they are enormously satisfying.

SO, JUST HOW BIG IS THE CANVAS?

I've never thought about this before, but I am curious to know what factors determine how the artist selects the size of canvas. Does the fee, time frame, genre, potential hanging space, or artist's vision determine the size? For an indexer, it is more likely that the editor or publisher determines how many pages are available for the index. Sometimes, given the text, it is a wholly inappropriate number whether on the plus or minus side. Unlike miniaturists who provide exquisite detail in small formats or abstract painters who produce blocks of single color on large canvases, the compositor has very little leeway in adjusting type size before the index becomes unreadable or a jarring counterpoint to the existing type size of the preceding text.

We may disagree, but I think it is more difficult to fill abundant index space for a content-light text than it is to craft a short index to content-rich text. With the former, one is repeating minute detail in all its synonymous forms. In the latter, one can only at best adopt an impressionist stance.

A WORD ABOUT VISUAL INTEGRITY

Although the content and purpose of a text primarily decide how exhaustive we need to be in our indexing, we can also exert some control to ensure the index is visually appealing.[5] By *appealing*, I mean that the index will be easy to use, allowing the reader to skim the columns quickly and automatically intuit clues to structure and organization. We can do this by means of concise but unambiguous wording, judicious use of capitalization and text styling, and index format (indented, run-in, or combination of the two), but rarely can we control the final layout parameters determined by the editor or book stylist. However, we can ensure that our effort adds to the user's experience: easy, fast, and accurate access.

YOU CAN TAKE THE INDEXER OUT OF THE PAINTING …

Not long ago, I thoroughly enjoyed a wonderful exhibit at the Metropolitan Museum of Art entitled *Rooms With a View: The Open Window in the 19th Century*. The foreground of the paintings often depicted the interior of the artists' studios or simple, hushed interiors with contemplative figures.[6] Sometimes the focal point was the window itself. As interesting and absorbing as the paintings were, largely by artists whose work was unfamiliar to me, all I could keep thinking about was, *How did they locate these? What was the keyword search? Who indexed the database?*

ENDNOTES

1. Frances Lennie and Alexander Nickerson, "Indexing Works: A *Key Words* Interview With Two Medical Indexers," in *Indexing Specialties: Medicine*, ed. L. Pilar Wyman (Medford, NJ: Information Today, Inc., 1999), 3–13.

2. Words do convey a publishing culture long passed. When I first started indexing in the 1970s, indexes were indeed "commissioned" for an offered set fee, I was pretty much left to my own devices, and the pace was leisurely. I was not "hired," and there were no discussions of page rates, no dictates from editor or author, and definitely no time crunch unless of my own making.

3. See images (including a few wonderfully misindexed images) at www.google.com/search?q=queen+elizabeth=2=portrait&hl=en&client=safari&tbo=u&rls=en&tbm=isch&source=univ&sa=X&ei=CyXFUNPmEqe0AGrloGABg&ved=0CC4QsAQ&biw=1236&bih=887.

4. See relevant sections in Hans H. Wellisch, *Indexing From A to Z*, 2nd ed. (New York: H. W. Wilson, 1996).

5. See Frances S. Lennie, "The Visual Appeal of Indexes: An Exploration," *The Indexer* 28, no. 2 (June 2010): 67–68.

6. See www.metmuseum.org/exhibitions/listings/2011/rooms-with-a-view.

Chapter 2

Creating Real-World Ecommerce Taxonomies: Getting Customers to Products

Fred Leise © 2014

Taxonomies are closely related to indexes. Both, after all, are controlled vocabularies whose purpose is to get users (readers/customers) to the information they want quickly and efficiently. However, especially in a retail setting, taxonomies are created and used in a much more collaborative way than an individual indexer does when facing a text alone.

This article will explore the creation of retail browsing taxonomies as an example of how such objects are created in the real world. This information will also serve as an introduction to taxonomy work for those indexers who may be interested in expanding their skills into that area.

DEFINITIONS

Controlled vocabularies (CVs) are any predetermined lists of words that are used for tagging content, enhancing search, or creating indexes. Controlled vocabularies come in three flavors: synonym rings, taxonomies, and thesauri.

Synonym rings are groups of words that are considered to be the same in a specific context. For example:

jeans = denim = blue jeans

Taxonomies are, strictly speaking, hierarchical structures of terms that include broader and narrower terms. For example, a geographic taxonomy could include (with regions as an optional level in the taxonomy):

continents > [regions] > countries > states > counties > cities.

In this case, two specific branches of the vocabulary might be:

Europe > Central Europe > Hungary > Pest > Budapest

North America > Canada > Manitoba > Winnipeg

Note, however, that in most business settings today, the term *taxonomy* has taken on the meaning of any controlled vocabulary, no matter which specific form of CV is being used.

Thesauri (singular: *thesaurus*) are CVs that are hierarchical taxonomies with the addition of related terms (RTs). For example:

appliances > small appliances > blenders RT food processors

In this example, *blenders* has the related term (RT) of *food processors*. Related terms are especially important in a retail setting, as they may drive cross-selling opportunities (i.e., alerting customers to related products they might also be interested in).

Retail browsing taxonomies are hierarchical structures consisting of types of products, which are used by website customers to find the specific products they are looking for or to explore the range of offerings of a specific retailer. The size of the taxonomy reflects the breadth and depth of that retailer's product assortment. J. C. Penney's website (jcp.com), for example, has just over 10 top-level categories (shown as tabs across the top of the page), while the Sears website (sears.com) has more than 25 top-level categories, as detailed on its site map (www.sears.com/shc/s/smv_10153_12605).

Wal-Mart exposes a three-level product browsing structure on its website, walmart.com (Figure 2.1). In this example, we can see the top-level category of *Electronics & Office*, the second level *Computers*, and the third level *Monitors*.

The Google product taxonomy (viewable via download at support.google.com/merchants/answer/1705911?hl=en) is an especially deep taxonomy, containing as many as seven levels:

Home & Garden > Kitchen & Dining > Tableware > Drinkware > Glassware > Stemware > Brandy Snifters

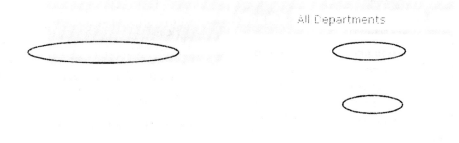

Figure 2.1 Wal-Mart's three-level product browsing structure

CREATING ECOMMERCE TAXONOMIES
Understanding Context
There are no universal CVs—in other words, none that apply in every possible circumstance. Even widely used CVs, such as the Dewey Decimal System of library classification, are specific to that particular context.

As Louis Rosenfeld and Peter Morville point out in *Information Architecture for the World Wide Web,* every information structure, including CVs, exists at the conjunction of a business context, a content context, and a user context (Figure 2.2).

Business Context
In the case of the retail browsing taxonomies, the business context is fairly clear: selling products to customers. Even here, however, there will be differences in the specific business context a retail company has. Is it selling a few high-end products to a few wealthy consumers, or is it a mass retailer selling literally millions of products to millions of customers? Compare the following two examples of the women's shoes taxonomy, the first from Prada and the second from Zappos:

Prada	**Zappos**
Pumps	Boots
Lace-ups	Heels
Loafers	Sandals
Slippers	Sneakers & Athletic Shoes
Sandals	Flats
Wedges	Clogs & Mules
	Loafers
	Slippers
	Oxfords
	Boat Shoes
	Insoles & Accessories
	Climbing

Also important in the business context is who owns the taxonomy. That is, who has ultimate responsibility for and the final say in the design of the CVs: the taxonomists who create the taxonomy, the merchants responsible for selling products, or perhaps even the marketing team?

Other factors in the business context come from the technical requirements or limitations inherent in a particular environment. All retail websites are fed from some type of database. Does that database allow polyhierarchies (taxonomies where a term can have multiple parents)? Does the database allow for infinite levels, or

Figure 2.2   Conjunction of a business context, a content context, and a user context

does it restrict the number of levels that a specific hierarchy can have? Does the database easily handle a faceted display of information, such as with Dow Corning's online product finder (dowcorning.com/applications/search/products)?

It is also important to understand how products get tagged so they are displayed in the proper place in the product hierarchy. Who does the tagging? In what system does the tagging happen? How is the taxonomy fed into that system? Finally, where does the product taxonomy itself live? Are there any limitations in that system?

All of these issues must be understood before a taxonomy can be designed. Otherwise, it might not be possible to implement the taxonomy as designed, resulting in a huge waste of time and effort.

Content Context

As previously noted, the size of the taxonomy will reflect the specific product assortment that the taxonomy is designed to classify. So anyone designing a retail taxonomy must understand the range of products being covered.

However, it is also important to create a taxonomy that is flexible enough to accommodate significant changes in product assortment. Retailers may acquire another company with different product assortments, or the retailer may decide to get out of an underperforming market. Any of these circumstances need to be reflected in a revised taxonomy.

User Context

Most important in any taxonomy project is the need to understand users and their mental models of the information space. If a product hierarchy will serve customers, enhancing their product finding and allowing them to more easily purchase products, it must reflect their terminology and mirror their mental model.

In most cases, those inside a retail company think about products in ways that are completely foreign to customers. For example, many retailers think about products in terms of hardlines or softlines. Yet a product hierarchy organized around those terms would be incomprehensible to the average customer.

The next section will explore how these contexts are elucidated during the creation process for a retail taxonomy.

Taxonomy Design Process

Stakeholder Interviews

To understand the business context for any taxonomy design project, it is important to conduct interviews with significant project stakeholders. Usually talking with five to eight individuals is enough to identify trends and commonalities in answers. Because there can be problems with leaders or more forceful individuals taking over a focus-group type session, these interviews work best when conducted on a one-on-one basis.

To keep on track during the interviews, use a predefined script, although the interviewer should feel free to follow up any particular answer off-script if that leads him to important information he would otherwise miss.

The questions in the interview script should focus on eliciting the following information:

1. What is the purpose of the project?

2. What pain point(s) is the project aimed at ameliorating?

3. Who are the important audiences for the project?

4. What will a successful project look like?

5. Are there any other ongoing or planned projects that will affect the taxonomy?

6. Are there any upcoming changes to the business, such as the addition or removal of product lines, that will affect the taxonomy?

7. Are there any major obstacles the project may face?

To help the interviewees feel at ease, it is a good idea to start with some general questions. For instance, ask what their title is, how long they have been in their current position, and what their major responsibilities are. The interviewer can then move to specific questions about the project at hand.

The script should use open-ended questions so that the interviewer doesn't lead the interview subject. For example, asking interviewees what their opinion is about the current taxonomy will yield more informative feedback than simply asking how well they like the current taxonomy. Of course, the interviewer can then ask a pair of questions about what the individual specifically likes and dislikes about the taxonomy. The open-ended question allows the interviewee to provide a more honest and useful initial response.

Stakeholder interviews should take anywhere from 30 minutes to an hour. Remember that stakeholders are busy individuals, so if the allotted interview time is up, the interviewer should offer to end the interview at that time. Schedule a follow-up session if absolutely necessary. Also, it is important to either take complete notes or record the interviews so you can have transcripts available for later use and reference.

After the interviews are complete, review the transcripts to identify patterns and commonalities in answers. Note also any conflicting information. This may indicate the need to get additional clarity about the project before proceeding.

Content Analysis

Content in an ecommerce setting will obviously be product-centered, and any retail CV must cover the breadth and depth of the product offerings. However, the content involved can be much more than just product titles and descriptions.

Large ecommerce sites now include much user-generated content (UGC). Such content may include reviews and recommendations, compiled lists, product videos, and more. How much of that content will the taxonomy cover? Does UGC need to be handled with a separate CV? Will it include (or use only) user-generated tags? TripAdvisor.com, for example, includes a "traveler type" facet for reviews, so you can isolate reviews for families, couples, solo travelers, or business travelers.

Answering those questions may require additional interviews with individuals responsible for creating or managing that content. But in any case, the taxonomist will need to perform a content audit or analysis.

In an audit, every piece of content is reviewed and recorded. Because of the size of a retailer's offerings, such an audit is usually impossible to perform. Instead, the taxonomist will need to perform a selective review of the types of product content available as well as the product types themselves, which will be included in the CV. It is helpful to interview merchandisers or buyers to determine whether any changes to the product mix are being contemplated. The proposed CV should accommodate those changes.

For extremely large retailers, the CV may be developed or revised by focusing on each single product line in turn, such as home furnishings, toys, clothing, shoes, or tools.

User Research

The ultimate users of the taxonomy are customers. If they can't understand the terminology, they can't find the products they are looking for and won't buy anything, which, after all, is the main purpose of an ecommerce website: enabling customers to purchase products.

There are a number of ways to investigate users' mental model of a particular retail space, such as one-on-one interviews, similar to stakeholder interviews, but with a specific focus on the product finding and purchasing process, or nondirected contextual enquiry, watching customers as they browse retail websites and purchase products on their own.

For taxonomy development, one of the important tools is the open card sort. This technique provides insight into how customers think about and group the products as well as how they name their groups. Essentially, users are presented with anywhere from 70 to 120 product images, with generic titles, and asked to (1) sort those images into groups that make sense to them and (2) name the groups they have created. It is often helpful to conduct a post-sort interview to obtain further insights into how the customers were thinking or to further explore any unusual or unclear results. By analyzing the results from eight to 10 customers from each audience segment, it is possible to discern patterns in grouping and group naming and to use those patterns to inform the CV development. One retailer I consulted with found that its customers were not able to define *fine jewelry*, so that potential category was dropped from its taxonomy.

Card sorting can be conducted in person or remotely, and card sorting tools range from an Excel spreadsheet to online commercially available testing websites. Most of the online websites have associated analysis tools that allow the viewing of co-occurrence spreadsheets or dendrite diagrams (branch-like structures that show term proximity). An excellent resource with further information about card sorting is Donna Spencer's book *Card Sorting: Designing Usable Categories*.

Taxonomy Validation

Using as input all of the various research activities, the taxonomy itself is developed, most often through an iterative process with reviews by relevant stakeholders. Such development can often take 3 or 4 weeks for taxonomies that cover large product collections.

The completed taxonomy should undergo an additional round of user testing at this point to be sure that what has been developed is understandable by actual users. If this is a taxonomy replacement or revision, it is helpful to perform A–B testing to be sure the new taxonomy performs at least as well as the old version. (In A–B testing, some customers are given the new taxonomy and some the old. They are then compared on how easily they can find a given list of specific products.)

DOCUMENTATION
Style Guide

To ensure consistency in large taxonomy projects, it is helpful to prepare a taxonomy style guide. This document should cover such topics as naming (including allowable and forbidden terms), term uniqueness requirements, grammatical forms of terms, compound terms (such as *Books and Magazines*), use of acronyms, and word order. It should also cover the specifics of term construction, such as use of singular vs. plural forms, use of ampersands, use of diacritical marks, use of serial commas, and treatment of fractions.

It is often helpful not just to describe the specific use cases for the taxonomy but also to include history notes that will provide later users of the guide with the reasons for specific decisions.

Process Documentation

Ecommerce taxonomies are not created in a vacuum; rather they happen in large, complex organizations. Accordingly, it is important to create a process document to ensure consistency among enterprise taxonomies. Such documentation should include both upstream stakeholders and downstream impacts (both systems and teams) that need to be informed of taxonomy changes. Good documentation will also include specifics of implementation strategies and processes.

As an example, consider this process from a fictional online retailer:

1.1 Buyer/merchandiser requests major taxonomy change

1.2 Taxonomy team receives request

1.3 Taxonomy team schedules and performs user testing

1.4 Taxonomy team analyzes testing results

1.5 Taxonomy team consults search engine optimization team

1.6 Taxonomy team consults marketing team

1.7 Taxonomy team revises taxonomy in an iterative process with buyers/merchandisers

1.8 Taxonomy team tests new taxonomy

1.9 Buyer/merchandiser approves final taxonomy

1.10 Taxonomy team informs the following for implementation of new taxonomy:

1.10.1 Information technology team

1.10.2 Mobile ecommerce team

1.10.3 Marketing team

1.10.4 Social marketing team

1.10.5 Digital asset management team

1.10.6 Search engine optimization/search engine marketing team

MAINTAINING ECOMMERCE TAXONOMIES

Ecommerce taxonomies are never finished. Rather they must change to reflect differing general language uses (think of *wireless* vs. *radio*) or alterations in the business itself. Plans must be put in place to ensure timely updates to product taxonomies. How does the taxonomy team get notified of changing product assortments that would result in the elimination or addition of parts of the taxonomy? Who makes the decision on which product line has priority when scheduling redesigns? How are new terms requested? How are term changes handled? How are errors such as misspellings handled?

Specific triggers for taxonomy reviews should also be defined. Most often these result from corporate acquisitions or splits, or the addition of entire product lines to a company's offerings.

Most importantly, it is necessary to define who is responsible for maintaining the taxonomy: a single individual, a self-contained team, or a committee drawn from multiple departments.

CONCLUSION

As we have seen, ecommerce taxonomies are highly complex constructs that directly affect a company's bottom line. Their construction requires considerable skill and experience. But those skills are a direct extension of an indexer's ability to determine both important concepts and the terminology that best expresses those concepts.

REFERENCES

The references that follow provide access to publications on thesaurus design specifically as well as customer-centric design in general.

Aitchison, Jean, Alan Gilchrist, and David Bawden. *Thesaurus Construction and Use: A Practical Manual*, 4th ed. London: Routledge, 2000.

Beyer, Hugh, and Karen Holtzblatt. *Contextual Design: Defining Customer-Centered Systems*. New York: ACM Press, 1998.

Constantine, Larry L., and Lucy A. D. Lockwood. *Software for Use: A Practical Guide to the Models and Methods of Usage-Centered Design*. New York: ACM Press, 1999.

Rosenfeld, Louis, and Peter Morville. *Information Architecture for the World Wide Web*. 3rd edition. Sebastopol, CA: O'Reilly & Associates, 2006.

Sacco, Giovanni Maria, and Yannis Tzitzikas, eds. *Dynamic Taxonomies and Faceted Search: Theory, Practice, and Experience*. New York: Springer Verlag, 2009.

Spencer, Donna. *Card Sorting: Designing Usable Categories*. New York: Rosenfeld Media, 2009.

Stewart, Darin L. *Building Enterprise Taxonomies*. Portland, OR: Mokita Press, 2008.

Young, Indi. *Mental Models: Aligning Design Strategy With Human Behavior*. New York: Rosenfeld Media, 2008.

Chapter 3

I Was a Teenage Taxonomist: The Light and Dark of Constructing Taxonomies at Bloomberg BNA

Chuck Knapp © 2014

It was already far too late, past midnight, and the air chilly. The wind in icy gusts sought the skin of my face and the gap between my hat and coat collar. It was a night to be indoors, and I hastened my pace, eager to reach my home. A shortcut, I thought, across the moors, could cut a half hour off my walk, even with the uncertain terrain. So I left behind the well-traveled road and struck off alone, unmindful of the mud on my boots and the racing of my heart. The off-road hiking was more strenuous, but the extra effort warmed me, I reasoned. It got the blood flowing. Despite the brightness of the moon, it was hard to see where I was going. A moist fog hovered across the moor, gathering in patches and then fading away again. Slogging my weary feet through ankle deep mud, my footsteps seemed thunderous in my own ears. The only other sound was my panting breath. Almost home, I thought. Just keep going.

I heard something. *What was that?!* I froze. At least I thought I heard something. A stick breaking or something moving. Motionless, I listened and looked around. The moon cast a pale blueness over the rocks and heath, sparkling puddles reflecting in the marsh all around. But the shadows hid far more than the moonlight revealed. Unseen creatures made their homes within the clumps of trees and bristly scrub. I got the feeling something was watching me. Something out there could see me. Something was stalking me.

I took two steps. I heard it move. I stopped. I faced the sound. Two red dots. Two fiery, hungry eyes. Behind it two more eyes, and two more. I dropped my bag and ran, but in seconds I felt myself knocked to the ground. An enormous weight pounced upon me. I felt my limbs pulled in different directions in violent jerks. A pack of fiendish taxonomists clawed at me and tore at my throat with their yellowish fangs. I fought them, in vain, overwhelmed by their ferocity. And then blackness, blackness, and more numb blackness. I lay there in darkness, alone. I have no idea how

15

much time passed. But when I opened my eyes there was a fuzzy greyness in the air, and I was floating in cold and damp and pain.

I gave thanks that it was over, even if I was dying. But it was not over. Unknown to me then, my terror had only begun. The fang marks on my neck throbbed in cruel testimony. Bitten by the pack, I was infected. And inside of me the hideous poison was already growing, making its way through my veins, transforming my very essence. It was only a matter of time now, but incontrovertibly I was on my way to becoming … a taxonomist.

Okay, I admit it. That is not exactly the way it happened. A pack of fiendish taxonomists did not hunt me down and bite me with their fangs. The truth is, after more than 16 years as a happy-go-lucky indexer, I was bit by the taxonomy bug, if I may be allowed to modify the metaphor. Since then, my life has not been the same. I underwent a transformation, and the following is a story of the important lessons I learned during that transformation.

In December 2008, in a span of two business days, I was asked if I could develop two different taxonomies. The first request came on a Friday afternoon from somebody new to our company. She was in marketing and wanted to "use taxonomy to better surface our tax products." The next Monday my director let me know that our president wanted to "explore further taxonomy" as a way for our subscribers to access our content. It felt like a calling.

Since my corporate surroundings would dictate the nature of my transformation from indexer to taxonomist, it is necessary to provide some introductory information about my company, Bloomberg BNA. Based in metropolitan Washington, D.C., we provide legal and business professionals with news and analysis. Our content covers various subjects including antitrust, employment law, environment, healthcare, securities, and tax. We number about 1,600 employees and have been a wholly owned subsidiary of Bloomberg since October 2011. Our Taxonomy and Indexing department has over 30 employees, all attorneys and subject matter experts dedicated to linking our subscribers with the information they need to do their jobs.

Not that the suspense was killing you, but I said yes to helping with the taxonomy projects, despite not ever actually having produced a taxonomy for hire before. I had taken taxonomy classes and workshops from some of the very best instructors. I had read articles and books by leading experts, but I had never created a taxonomy outside of a class. But 16 years of indexing experience does count for something. It was enough to get me started. And as in so much in life, getting started was the most important part.

A SINISTER TRANSFORMATION, OUT OF CONTROL: A NEW WAY OF THINKING

This great change was taking hold of me, but for weeks and months it went unnoticed. To most of my co-workers and friends, I appeared exactly the same. Outwardly, I looked just like the indexer I had always been. I walked among them as I always had, during daylight hours. They had no reason to question, "Could an indexer become a taxonomist?" Indeed, it is hard for non-indexers to see exactly what the difference is between the two.

The fact is, a good indexer can become a good taxonomist—and a bad indexer can even become a bad taxonomist. Many of the crucial skill sets are exactly the same. You must accurately describe and classify the content involved. And you must also anticipate the needs and inclinations of the user trying to access that information. Being good with words, and being good with organization, are also essential. Both taxonomists and traditional indexers need to avoid imprecise terminology and unclear relationships between concepts.

For taxonomy, it is all about the structure. For traditional indexes, alphabetical order and cross-references are what guide users. Taxonomy is less forgiving, in that every term must fit somewhere within the hierarchy. It must follow the broader-to-narrower tree structure. Narrower terms (NTs) must fit entirely within their broader terms (BTs). Overlap is the enemy. Sibling terms at each level must be harmonious. There are lots of rules to follow. Flat indexes must also follow rules and a logical consistent structure, of course. But so long as A is followed by B, and C by D, indexing permits a little more wiggle room about including different concept types side-by-side.

These basic differences loomed large in my own mind. The rest of the world seemed to regard them as subtle details of the sort that I and my crew dealt with on a daily basis, but they were very content to leave that to us. And so we were turned loose on these two different taxonomy projects. Both were clearly defined but with very different goals, and both were aimed at serving the needs of our company to assist subscribers or attract potential subscribers.

The dual taxonomy projects each benefited the other, but they were very different. The marketing taxonomy was smaller. It needed to be finished in a couple of months, and we knew we wanted the terms at its lowest level to correspond with what amounted to a catalog of all our tax publications. Fortunately, our new marketing director had "done lots of taxonomies" and brought expertise and confidence enough to get us started on our way. She also provided sage advice and helped with the inevitable close-call choices. It was developed quickly, in successive iterations with fairly continuous feedback. Each draft brought us closer to what was envisioned. We focused more on searcher expectations than library science, and we did not get too hung up on sticky, complicated concepts so long as there was a clear and understandable path to each term.

The other project took a more ambitious scope and required over two years to complete. The assignment was to create a topical thesaurus of all of Bloomberg BNA's content that would be searchable and browsable by subscribers. For both projects, we would have to select software to serve our needs, develop a consistent process and philosophy, and cultivate the expertise necessary to achieve our goals. Our indexing background provided a great advantage. I only realized how much through interactions with companies that do not have their own indexing departments. Very simple things indexers take for granted after working in the field for years can be a struggle for those without that experience.

Mining for terms to use in a taxonomy is a crucial early step. Years' worth of BNA index headings provided a wealth of good options to start with, and a huge leg up. Our indexes, going all the way back to the 1931 *U.S. Law Week* index, are made up of subject headings that group together more specific subentries. These headings are all nouns or adjective-noun phrases (e.g., *executive compensation*), exactly as needed for taxonomy. They also represent properly sized buckets. Over the years, our indexers developed a good feel for the proper level of necessary detail. So yes, we stole like bandits from these indexes wherever we could. Often, exact index headings resided unchanged side-by-side with other index headings, now as topics in our ever-growing taxonomy. These signposts of familiarity were no doubt a comfort to editors throughout the company but also probably further delayed widespread realization that any major change was afoot. But the work we were undertaking was indeed very different, and accomplishing it would require very different tools.

A MOB OF ANGRY PEASANTS, ARMED WITH PITCHFORKS AND TORCHES: COLLABORATION

The single most dramatic difference between taxonomy development and indexing work, in my experience, has been the premier role of collaboration. Why this is so very true, I am not certain. But true it is. Collaboration has been the defining characteristic throughout every taxonomy I have helped develop. In order to get it just right, you need input from subject matter experts, end users, and those who are applying the taxonomy topics as metadata as well as all other stakeholders. Early in my indexing career, I heard indexing described as an ivory tower kind of profession. It was for introverts, comfortable for hours alone with a computer screen or the printed page. The majority of us probably do fall most comfortably into this category. But this will not work for taxonomy development.

Caue solo taxonomist! Or as they might say in Transylvania, "*păze‚te-te tax-onomist solo!*" Beware the solo taxonomist! No matter how brilliant she is working alone in a mountaintop laboratory beneath a lightning-streaked sky, she will create something that will not work for you, or at the very least, needs an overhaul. Stories abound. But I remember attending a taxonomy event[1] at the Library of Congress where a presenter recounted how his company had hired a taxonomist who worked round-the-clock full-time for a year. One year later, the hired taxonomist presented his masterpiece. There were several acrimonious exchanges. Stakeholders walked out of the meeting. The expert taxonomist was fired. And the new taxonomist, the current presenter, was brought in to salvage the situation.

This is not to say that if you work for yourself, you cannot offer your services to develop a taxonomy. Sure you can. A single person can create a fantastic taxonomy. You just need to make sure you do not work in a vacuum but, instead, get input at every stage from stakeholders and subject experts. At the beginning, get guidance that is as sharply focused as possible. But present a very rough draft early before you go too deep. Give stakeholders that straw man to react to. Let them poke holes in it and kick it around. Listen to them and make adjustments. Taxonomists need to be very iterative. Create a draft and show it. Refine it and show it again. Refine it again and show it again. When finished, the taxonomy should not be the taxonomist's alone, but should represent input from all the stakeholders.

Be flexible. Taxonomists cannot grow so attached to their creation that they are unwilling to change it. If, like Doctor Frankenstein, we are shown that our creation is flawed and beginning to cause some trouble, we need to take steps to change it before it runs amok. In the long run, studying user behavior will be a good way to discover the need for refinements once the taxonomy is in use. But during creation, a taxonomist should get as much input from subject matter experts and others as possible. Involving non-taxonomists means you should be prepared to provide some education. In fact, you had better get used to educating over and over again. You may feel like a broken record. A taxonomist will also have to explain choices made—repeatedly—without getting defensive. This can be frustrating when under deadline pressure, but it is entirely necessary. Remember, it is just part of the job. Keep a script to repeat if you need to. Embrace being a teacher.

One tool I used that helped was a two-page taxonomy introduction primer that I wrote and reused each time a new group was asked to provide feedback on a taxonomy branch. It outlined what we were trying to do in very basic terms, using language and examples commonly understood around my company. Providing that common footing at the very start saved a lot of time. Collaboration is key to a taxonomy's strength. But throughout the back-and-forth around-the-table exchange, we must remember also another axiom of controlled vocabulary: "Input from many. Control by few."

A MONSTER, FEARED AND REVILED: THE WORD "NO"

Perhaps a taxonomist's most important job is to say no. More is not better. Not everything can go into the taxonomy. Saying no will not make you popular, but you have to be firm. The integrity and usefulness of the taxonomy matter more than whether everybody likes you. Input from many but control by a few forms the essence of vocabulary control, but it is bound to lead to disappointment.

Given the importance of collaboration as well as professional relationships with colleagues you rely upon on an ongoing basis, however, it is much better if you can avoid being universally regarded as a "no"-spewing monster. You do not want everyone to hate and attack the taxonomy, after all. Probably the best way to minimize unpopularity is to go one step further and say, "No, *and here's why not.*" Taking time to explain why adding a term would be problematic, or why that phrasing would create confusion or inconsistency, can make the difference between winning over a taxonomy supporter or creating a taxonomy enemy.

Regrettably, this is something we did not do as thoroughly as we would like to have done throughout the creation phase of the Bloomberg BNA taxonomy. Our team's open call for suggestions was somewhat naive. We were quite soon overwhelmed, and we were not able to keep up with every single emailed suggestion. Some people offering input grew understandably dissatisfied at the lack of response. What we failed at initially, we hope to correct now that our taxonomy is complete. A feedback loop system is a major component of the second phase of our taxonomy maintenance. Its primary focus is to provide a transparent tool that educates and explains each time a suggestion is made. If you expect ongoing requests of more than a couple dozen a week, you will probably want to institute a system to help.

Returning to talk of enemies, I was once part of a phone conference involving participants from different cities. Dialing in, we did not enter the access code quickly enough and were routed to the main switchboard. When we said we were trying to join the taxonomy meeting, we were questioned, "The taxenemy meeting?" We had never heard that one before and it tickled us, the idea of taxenemies out there trying to thwart us. Two points to make from this. First, we do want to avoid taxenemies. Someone attacking your taxonomy whenever you turn around is bad for everyone. Second, long-distance communication presents challenges. When in-person brainstorming is impossible, it is easy to drift into a back-and-forth exchange dynamic that can trend toward an us-versus-them mentality. A taxonomist may labor for days to create something perfect and then present it to a subject matter expert for comments. The subject matter expert may then spend days formulating iron-clad arguments for changes and present them. The taxonomist then says no. If this happens more than once, change the approach. Shift from email to telephone if it is not possible to meet in person. As much as possible, get the various stakeholders to make the tricky decisions together.

THE BIBLE AND THE GREATEST WEAPON TO WARD OFF EVIL: FOLLOW THE RULES

Your greatest defense when working on a taxonomy project will be the bible. By "bible," I mean of course, the ANSI/NISO Z39.19-2005.[2] It is the nearly 200-page standard for controlled vocabularies. It will provide guidance in times of dissension and comfort in times of tribulation. It also provides justification. Internationally recognized standards carry more credibility, it turns out, than "because I say so." Every taxonomist should keep a copy handy and be prepared to quote from it or even thrust it with outstretched arms into the face of a tormentor. It will hold them at bay.

If you are new to taxonomy, by all means carefully read through the ANSI/NISO standard. You may not necessarily want to read it end-to-end in one sitting—it is more of a reference book than an instructional manual—but you will find many answers there, so you need to be familiar with it. Fortunately, it has an outstanding index. For new taxonomists, I would urge particular attention to the sections on term choice, scope, and form. The section on purpose, concepts, principles, and structure is equally key. And no doubt you will want to read the glossary and introduction.

Why follow the standard? There are many reasons, but some big ones are:

- It makes sense.

- It ensures the taxonomy will work.

- It promotes interoperability and mergeability with other taxonomies should the need arise.

- It is already there (i.e., there is no need to entirely reinvent the wheel).

Experienced taxonomists do not need to be told all this. And I suspect they have learned, as I did, of the standard's persuasive powers when they had to mediate between disagreeing parties. As mentioned before, we are called upon to educate non-taxonomists time and time again. My own taxonomy team derived a measure of mirth from just how predictably I would fall back on the standard in times of distress. They never knew whether it would be 10 minutes into a meeting or 45. But they expected every time that it was only a matter of time before I uttered the term *ANSI/NISO* to their great delight. They actually made a drinking game out of it. As soon as it was uttered, they would all simultaneously grab their water bottles and coffee mugs and drink a gulp. (No adult beverages were involved. We did not have *that* much fun, at least as far as I know.) But do not be afraid to wield the standard as a weapon of defense. Non-taxonomists will respect it, and they will ultimately have more confidence in the taxonomy knowing that it adheres to recognized best practices.

Taxonomy work relies on many rules. The rules help. We should follow the rules. When I break rules, it almost always comes back to bite me. At the very least it comes back to haunt me. Most taxonomy software helps with this. The software typically enforces at least some of the basic rules. For example, the software will not allow you to use a single term for multiple meanings. It will enforce that each term's relationships remain constant. Should a term be polyhierarchical, the term will mean the exact same thing at both of its locations within the taxonomy. I know some people create taxonomies using spreadsheets or without software. My hat is off to them. But I simply could not work that way, at least with any taxonomy exceeding a hundred terms or so. In addition to the help you get from a taxonomy software's enforcement of taxonomy rules, it is also a more efficient way to work. Considering the time and resources that go into taxonomy development and maintenance, it is worthwhile to invest in reliable software. My company uses MultiTes (www.multites.com) and has been very satisfied with it.[3] It is reasonably priced, and with a few clicks, you can easily output your thesaurus in a variety of formats including XML, HTML, delimited text, and SKOS.

GOOD REALLY DOES TRIUMPH IN THE END: BE VIRTUOUS

The seven heavenly virtues have been set forth as chastity, temperance, charity, diligence, patience, kindness, and humility.[4] They seem pretty hard, though, so let us just try for three of them. We do not want to be accused of being overambitious. Diligence, patience, and humility make a much shorter list, and all are key for taxonomy construction.

Diligence is what will determine the quality of your taxonomy. Only through constant, careful effort can you produce a high-quality product. Shortcuts do not really exist. This is not to say you must agonize over every single term or decision. Sometimes, it is just fine to put a placeholder term in there or a placeholder structure. There is nothing wrong with that so long as you recognize you will eventually have to circle back to it. Use the placeholder for a little while until something better occurs to you. Sometimes you will have to shoehorn a term where it does not fit perfectly, until you come up with something better. The common joke among taxonomists is that they are always being asked when the taxonomy will be finished. The chorus-like unison response is, "It is never finished," most often spoken with a blend of gloom and glee. Our work is never done. It must be continuously reviewed and refined. If a taxonomy is left untended, it will grow less useful. That fact needs to be recognized by stakeholders, and reinforced by taxonomists.

Do not think you have to come up with every brilliant solution yourself. If that were the case, my own taxonomy career would have ended mere moments after it started. Feedback from taxonomy users will often be the very best source of ideas for refinement. Sometimes you need to just get something out there in order to spur some better ideas. Perfection does not need to be attained with the first idea you try. But the overall structure needs to be sound. If you knowingly create a structure based on fuzzy logic, uncertain relationships, or ambiguous terminology, you are headed for disaster. Be diligent and it will show in the taxonomy.

Patience will prove essential during taxonomy development. As mentioned, collaboration and education are ongoing components. Non-taxonomists who do not eat and breathe taxonomy every day will always have questions. It is merely the nature of the beast. Each time you explain a decision, you get practice for the next time, even if the repetition can wear on your nerves. Perseverance is an aspect of patience you must also exercise in order to get everything just right, as alluded to earlier.

Taxonomy governance also demands patience. Many of the worst mistakes I have made, and still make, stem from a rush to judgment. Most frequently this rush arises from a desire to be responsive and quickly address a problem. Often the best of intentions have spurred this unwise haste; we want to please somebody who is asking for a change. This was another area where my team hurt our own effort by creating unhelpful expectations. During the taxonomy creation phase, we were very fortunate to have no technical limitations on when we could make taxonomy changes. Because we had the ability to quickly effect changes, we often would wow our co-workers by making them very quickly. The result was that if we did not make a change very soon after somebody requested it, they resented it. Folks grew to expect a change to be made within hours or even minutes of a request. It was a monster of our own creation, and though it has not destroyed us, it still bedevils us. We would have done much better to establish early a cycle for regular and scheduled changes. Let the requester, as well as the governance group, sleep on it for awhile. I would even go so far as to urge depersonalizing, to some extent, the change request system. The worst possible scenario would be that anyone regard taxonomy changes as personal favors granted quickly on a whim. A taxonomy governance group should take its time, weigh all considerations, and then calmly make a reasoned and deliberate decision. Patience is key to making the right decisions.

Humility is the most important virtue of all. Show-offs make lousy taxonomists. Our work product must appear simple and obvious to all who use it. We will never dazzle or thrill with our creation. The biggest compliment a user can pay a taxonomy might be, "Well, duh." The trained eye may recognize its genius, but most will just pass through it on their way to what they were looking for. We must content ourselves with being useful rather than admired. For those who lack humility that may not be enough reward.

The worst taxonomies I have seen were created by people who needed to impress others with how smart they were. Just as we learn from the best taxonomies, we can also learn from the worst. It is good to study a bad taxonomy now and again. Arcane language, very subtle distinctions, elaborate structures, or extreme detail are often indicators that a taxonomy has been designed to serve the taxonomist's vanity rather than its intended beneficiaries. If a user needs an instruction manual to follow your taxonomy, you have probably failed. I remember a colleague's first full day of taxonomy work several years ago at the very beginning of our project. He devoted about 7 hours that day to drafting a branch on corporate governance. It was his first attempt, and at the end of the day, he printed off a copy and laid it on the desk for the two of us to study. We stared for a minute or two at the single sheet of paper with about a dozen words on it. I was no more an expert taxonomist than he was. After a while he broke the silence. "I know," he confessed, "it does not look like much."

"No, no, no," I assured him. "It's fine." We were both coming to grips with a new fact. The crowning glory to a successful day of work for a taxonomist would always be, at best, the following: You would labor extensively and agonize over choices and revisions. After many scratch-outs, you would often arrive at something that was still less than 100 percent perfect in your eyes. All this effort was in hope of ending up with something that looks as if a teenager could have tossed it together in 5 minutes without thinking. Simplicity was the ultimate goal. The ultimate reward was to take extremely complicated and often complex concepts, and then present them in a fashion that results in the reaction, "Yeah (*shrug*), that's what I would have done."

Bigger is not better. Every taxonomy serves different needs, but if a taxonomist boasts of how many thousand terms his taxonomy contains, he might again be motivated by the wrong needs. But it is a pretty understandable outcome given the influences out there. The second-most common question from bosses behind *Is it done yet?* would be *How much is done?* Almost as dangerous as the person who needs to prove how smart they are is the person who needs to prove how hard they have been working. That single page with 12 words on it at the end of the day is much less impressive than hundreds and hundreds of terms to the untrained eye. Too many in the business world have been trained to equate volume of output with success. Resist the impulse to churn out as many terms or branches as possible. Humility must prevail over the need for grandiosity.

NO SILVER BULLET: OVERSELLING WHILE TRYING TO SHOW VALUE

Investing in taxonomy can require significant resources and have broad impact across numerous departments in a company. The first step in taxonomy development is justifying even undertaking such a project. Of course, you want to be successful in making the case for taxonomy, but it is possible my group was a tad too successful. In holding forth taxonomy as the means of achieving so many corporate goals, we saddled it with pretty significant pressure. That pressure had the effect of amplifying the importance of every decision and often led to hard-fought battles over minutiae. Discourse is good, but one does not want to be paralyzed by sides digging in too deep in opposition to each other over every detail. Exclusion of a term from the taxonomy was equated with invisibility. This feeling was all the more difficult to dispel because we did not yet have a functioning subscriber-facing taxonomy we could show to everyone. It was still under development so we were limited to wireframes aimed at illustrating how the taxonomy one day would function.

Eventually, we found ourselves back-pedaling to play down taxonomy's role as corporate messiah. We had to re-establish a realistic perspective for our company. We had to argue the case that taxonomy was not the *only* way a user could access content. We had to emphasize that taxonomy was primarily a structure to aid searchers by allowing them to drill down to narrower topics. Our taxonomy branch review and vetting process, by necessity, emphasized navigating through a tree structure. And some users no doubt will explore content by browsing that way. But we still presume 90 percent of users will start with a simple search. Every single piece of content did not require its own taxonomy topic. A text search for a very specific item would still return results for that item. Users would still find it. It was not rendered invisible by not being repeated in the taxonomy. It did not serve the overall structural integrity of the taxonomy to design around the oddball concepts. Taxonomy is merely a structure that enables a greatly improved utilization of our content.

POWER UNLEASHED ON AN UNSUSPECTING WORLD: WHAT IT CAN DO AND WHAT YOU CAN DO

But let us not downplay the power of taxonomy too much. If knowledge is power, then certainly accessing information is as crucial now as it ever was. We live in an information age. We are surrounded by arguably too much information, and the challenge has become sifting through the unwanted bits to more quickly arrive at what is relevant. Professional indexers embracing taxonomy is one way to ensure our ongoing relevance. By taking our work behind-the-scenes to aid searchers, we are actually getting much closer to our end users than ever before. This is true whether they fully understand what is going on or not. Today's researcher expects to type in a word and go. Taxonomy utilizes indexers' skill and effort to make that experience as easy and rewarding as possible for the user.

At Bloomberg BNA, we are using our taxonomy to insert metadata in every news story as it is published online. This not only enables topical access to our content, it allows subscribers to customize how they receive our content based on preferred topic choices. Our indexers are busy tagging up stories as long as the news desk is open and releasing material. Each indexer/tagger monitors publishing queues in their areas of subject expertise. When notified of a story's readiness, they immediately read it and classify it according to appropriate topics.[5]

These topic tags also provide links between related documents to increase awareness of ongoing developments. Some products use taxonomy to organize their user interface by filtering content to topic-based tabs arranged across the top of the screen. Now that Bloomberg BNA is part of the larger Bloomberg company, taxonomy is part of how we will integrate our content with that of Bloomberg Law and other Bloomberg subsidiaries. More opportunities are in development. We have only scratched the surface.

Looking outside my own company, it is obvious that taxonomy is on the rise. The American Society for Indexing (ASI) has a Special Interest Group for Taxonomies & Controlled Vocabularies (www.taxonomies-sig.org). More recently, the Special Libraries Association (SLA) created a Taxonomy Division (taxonomy.sla.org). And Taxonomy Boot Camp (www.taxonomybootcamp.com) has attracted hundreds of participants each year since 2005 and gets bigger every year. Taxonomists are in demand.

In the past four years that I have worked as a taxonomist, I have learned numerous lessons. I learned the importance of collaboration as well as the importance of saying no. I also saw how much was to be gained through following the rules and proceeding with diligence, patience, and humility. I learned to embrace simplicity. The most important lesson I learned during my transformation from indexer to taxonomist was, quite simply, that I could do it. I also learned that I like it. If anything, it has made me a better indexer. And I learned that an indexing career is great preparation for a taxonomy career. And just like a good horror movie, the door is wide open for a series of sequels.

ENDNOTES

1. Taxonomy Tuesdays, a mostly monthly gathering of Washington, D.C. taxonomists to discuss issues and experiences.

2. ANSI/NISO Z39.19-2005, Guidelines for the Construction, Format, and Management of Monolingual Controlled Vocabularies, available at www.niso.org/apps/group_public/download.php/6487/Guidelines%20for%20the%20Construction,%20Format,%20and%20Management%20of%20Monolingual%20Controlled%20Vocabularies.pdf.

3. Since 1983, MultiTes has offered thesaurus management tools and has enhanced them as new technology and standards are developed.

4. Aurelius Clemens Prudentius identified seven virtues in his *Psychomachia* (*Battle for Man's Soul*), written in AD 410.

5. For a description of BBNA's transition from indexing to live tagging, see Dena Shorago, "Tag, You're It!" *Indexers Ink: The Newsletter of the Pacific-Northwest Chapter of the American Society of Indexing* (Fall/Winter 2010), pnwasi.org/indexing/wp-content/uploads/2012/06/2010_fall.pdf.

Chapter 4

Ebook Indexing

Glenda Browne and Mary Coe © 2014

Ebook indexing has recently moved from being a field for specialists to being mainstream. Most professional indexers will have to learn how to index for ebooks, if they are not doing so already. This will include working with some ebooks derived as an afterthought from print books (pbooks), and many more that will be "born" digital with content designed for ebook publication from the beginning. Existing print content that is being converted retrospectively is known as legacy content.

In this chapter, we focus on ebooks for portable ereaders. We provide background information on ebook formats and readers; discuss the current status of ebook indexing and future possibilities; give an overview of some of the software programs that may be used for ebook indexing; and offer suggestions of ways in which we need to adapt our indexing for variable-sized screens. We also cover book-level metadata and conclude with ideas on future options for ebook indexes. Primarily, we will be discussing reflowable ebooks that are designed to be read on portable devices of various sizes, and we will also touch on fixed-format ebooks.

Reflowable ebooks are those that don't rely on page numbers (although they may retain them) and reformat to fit the size of the device on which they are being read or to the preferences of the user. Because words can automatically wrap to the next line, the amount of text displayed on the screen will vary for different devices and font sizes. Because of this variance, there is no generalizable concept of a "page" in reflowable ebooks, and there is no guarantee that different items (e.g., figures and tables) that were viewed next to each other on a print page will appear together on a screen. As pages have constituted the basis of most pbook indexes, this requires us to think about index locators differently.

Fixed-format ebooks (usually PDFs), on the other hand, retain the same layout no matter what device they are read on. Most often, they are read on computer screens; when viewed on portable reading devices, the reader usually has to scroll to see a whole page.

EBOOK FORMATS AND EBOOK READERS

EPUB is the international standard format for trade ebooks. It is a free and open ebook standard developed by the International Digital Publishing Forum (IDPF). It is based on, and supersedes, the Open eBook standard (OEB) that had been created by the Open eBook Forum (now IDPF) in 1999 as a standard for reflowable ebooks.

EPUB uses existing, open standards wherever possible (e.g., CSS and XHTML, which are also used on the web). The IDPF EPUB Indexes Working Group has been formed to develop a standard for indexes (more about this group in a later section). The Book Industry Study Group has released an EPUB 3 Support Grid (bisg.org/what-we-do-12-152-epub-30-support-grid.php) that shows the various ereader devices by the EPUB 3 features they support. IDPF and supporters have also developed an ereading system called Readium (readium.org) that aims to be fully EPUB 3-compliant.

EPUB 3 focuses on accessibility and incorporates the requirements of the DAISY talking book standard.[1] EPUB documents use semantic markup, which means that coding (using XHTML tags) describes what things are, rather than how they should be displayed. For example, a subentry will be coded as such, rather than just showing as indented text. Semantic markup and consistent structure make EPUB documents easier to navigate, as actions can be based on predictable features. For example, if footnotes are tagged, a reader can choose to hide them and only see the main text.[2]

Portable Document Format (PDF) has in the past served as the main standard for fixed-format ebooks; however, for born-digital books, publishers also have the option of creating fixed-format ebooks based on HTML. There is an IDPF working group investigating advanced/hybrid fixed layouts; these will combine some of the benefits of both reflowable text and fixed formats.

Amazon Kindle readers use a proprietary format, meaning that Kindle books have to be read on Kindle ereaders or using a Kindle app for computers. Older Kindle readers use the proprietary format, AZW or .mobi, based on the Mobipocket standard, while newer ones have Kindle Format 8 (KF8). The Kindle standard is based on a type of XHTML, which means that it is not that different from EPUB. Amazon has not encouraged indexes in ebooks, saying "Indexes are not recommended at this time."[3]

Amazon's X-Ray function (available on Kindle Touch) provides a sparkline graph (series of lines of different thicknesses) showing occurrences of names (and other topics) throughout the book.[4]

Obooks (online books) in libraries are made available in large collections, in some cases searchable in combination with periodical literature and other information resources. They may be presented in PDF format or HTML and are usually read on computer screens or printed.

PAGES, PARAGRAPHS, OR POINTS

The loss of meaningful pages in ebooks with reflowable content has major implications for indexes, for which locators have usually come from the page numbers. The loss of consistent page numbers has led publishers to create ineffective indexes for ebooks. Fixed-format documents have fared better, as print indexes can be converted to linked indexes that connect the user to the correct page. While page numbers might remain in use for at least some time (for citation and comparison purposes), they will not be the most significant locators for ebooks, especially when compared to sections, paragraphs, or precise locations in the text.

The advantages and disadvantages of various types of locators have been discussed in the literature:[5]

- Page numbers are useful for citation and comparison purposes (when people with different formats wish to refer to the same text). They also sometimes offer the easiest solution for books converted from print with print indexes leading to page numbers. Print metaphors still carry meaning to the reader (e.g., depth or range of discussion), and we may not want to lose them completely.

- Paragraph and section numbers usually provide smaller targets for index links, although sections can be larger than one print-equivalent page. They can be quicker to index to than precise locations, and embedded indexing may be better preserved and more readily translated at the paragraph level. They may also provide the context around the precise information being targeted.

- Precise targets in the text take the user immediately to the exact location required. They may be the best approach for individual topics that are exactly named in the text.

- Other options, such as chapter and verse for biblical content or question numbers for workbooks, might be considered for specific works.

Embedded indexing (discussed a little later in this chapter) enables single sourcing, allowing the provision of page numbers for pbook indexes and links to specific locations for ebooks or obooks. Page ranges also need to be considered. The simplest solution is to link to the beginning of a discussion, but showing the start and end points of a discussion can make the index more usable, by enabling the reading system to provide information about the indexed text (e.g., highlighting the range with a colored background) and for the new Index Locator Search feature proposed by the EPUB Indexes Working Group.

WHY EBOOKS NEED INDEXES

The publishing community is divided between those who believe that the search function can replace indexes, and those who look forward to the day when quality ebook indexes become the norm. Providing users with the most efficient ways to search, browse, and use indexes allows them to choose the access method most useful and comfortable to them.

Why do we need indexes as well as search? Fundamentally, indexes are explorable documents. They simultaneously provide an overview of a document and direct access to information on specific topics. The gathering of broad and narrow concepts and related terms within indexes, and their concise presentation, are two things that set them apart from lists of search results. Indexes provide a level of granularity between that of a table of contents and a set of search results, and this is often what users require. James Lamb asked the question "Why have a human-produced index where full text searching is available?" and identified the following features of human-based indexing:[6]

- Homographs can be distinguished through the use of parenthetical qualifiers.

- Synonyms can be collocated using *See* references or double entries.

- Trivial content (passing mentions) can be omitted from the index.

- Inferences can be indexed.

- Graphics can be indexed using words that describe the content and the meaning it adds to the text.

Peter Meyers considers the same question and adds that indexes:[7]

- Provide guided discovery by creating clusters of related topics.

- Help when you know what you want, but aren't sure how to describe it.

- Signal depth of coverage.

- Provide a one-stop tally of coverage points throughout a book.

- Help prospective buyers evaluate a book.

Jan Wright summed it all up when she said, in her 2012 presentation at the WritersUA conference, "until a computer can complete the New York Times crossword puzzle, with all of its puns, triple meanings, and jokes, indexers are needed because machines still don't get what we are doing with words and wordplay of all kinds."

EBOOK INDEXES OF THE PAST

While ebook formats have worked well for fiction and other texts that are read linearly, they have less success with nonfiction books, where the ability to move backward and forward through the work is crucial, and where complex formatting (e.g., tables, sidebars, and figures) makes this difficult. The loss of page numbers in reflowable texts increases the difficulty in adapting print indexes for the ebook environment, and many publishers have not developed the procedures necessary for the inclusion of useful, active indexes in books with reflowable text. Publishers' approaches to date have been to:

- Omit indexes.

- Include terms from pbook indexes without page numbers (an "index without legs").

- Include indexes from pbook versions without linking them, with page numbers that have no relevance in reflowable text, suggesting that these entries might provide useful ideas for search terms.

- Include fully linked indexes using embedded indexing or linking, either done in-house or using an ebook production company. Unfortunately, even when the links work, these indexes do not always display appropriately (e.g., with turnover lines outdenting further to the left than main entries).[8]

An informal study of Amazon Kindle ebooks found that of 21 titles that had indexes in print form, only two had fully functional, linked indexes in the ebook. When Amazon says that a book includes an index, it is not easy to find out in advance whether it is an active, linked index or just a reproduction of the print-format index.[9]

EBOOK INDEX ADVOCACY

Because ebook publishers have not always included effective indexes in ebooks, the indexing societies have taken the role of advocates. These societies and individual indexers have advocated within the standards, publishing, and technology communities for the inclusion of quality, active indexes in ebooks.

The American Society for Indexing (ASI) Digital Trends Task Force (DTTF) was established in May 2011. It has:

- Established a LinkedIn group with a collection of useful links and discussions (tinyurl.com/ASIDTTFLinkedIn).

- Made contact with technology companies to discuss requirements for ebook indexing using programs such as Adobe InDesign and FrameMaker.

- Attended teleconferences of the National Information Standards Organization (NISO) Ebook Special Interest Group (SIG; tinyurl.com/NISOebookSIG).

- Been instrumental in the formation of the IDPF EPUB Indexes Working Group (discussed later in this chapter).

- Attended digital publishing, librarian, technical writing, and ebook conferences to present sessions on ebook indexing.

- Developed prototypes of ebook index interfaces and index mashups.

- Converted ASI books into ebooks, focusing on active working ebook indexes as models.

- Presented ebook sessions at chapter meetings and national society meetings to educate indexers about the challenges and tools to use for ebook indexing.

The Society of Indexers has also been active in this area, establishing a Publishing Technology Group to advocate for quality indexes and to inform publishers and indexers.[10] *The Indexer* journal published a collection of articles for beginners collected from *The Indexer*. This collection has an active index in both Kindle and EPUB formats, thus providing a good example of what can be done.[11] Lamb has written about practical issues that arise when converting the text and linking the index at paragraph level.[12] The Australian and New Zealand Society of Indexing (ANZSI) has joined the IDPF and participated in the Indexers Working Group and has gathered useful links about ebook indexing on their website (www.anzsi.org/site/ebooks.asp).

IDPF AND THE EPUB INDEXES WORKING GROUP

IDPF is a community-based organization that develops and maintains the EPUB standard. EPUB publications are zipped collections of resources that can be interpreted by reading systems and rendered (displayed) for users. Some of these resources provide metadata and navigation information, while others hold the actual content.[13]

A new feature in EPUB 3 is the Canonical Fragment Identifier (CFI). CFIs are automatically generated pointers to every part of the text, which enable links to connect to every part of a document without the target markers having to be added individually. They describe every location in a book through its relationship to the start of the book. CFIs are important as they act as potential anchors for links from indexes, but they are not easily human readable, and we do not as yet have software to easily insert them into indexes.

IDPF established an EPUB Indexes Working Group (code.google.com/p/epub-revision/wiki/IndexesMainPage) in 2012, following a submission from the ASI DTTF. Members include indexers, publishers, and technology companies.[14]

Expert Tip

The upcoming EPUB specification is expected to enable the creation of basic chapter-like indexes as well as allowing searching of the index from within the text and the display of index terms associated with selected sections of the text.

A use case for a basic index (called the chapter-like index) and implementation ideas developed by the group include:

- Index term search (pop-up index): Search from within the text, either by highlighting words in the text or typing the search term.

- Index locator search: Retrieve all index entries that are attached to a highlighted range of text.

- Standalone index: Ebooks that contain nothing but indexes to other ebooks (e.g., journal collections or books in series).

While EPUB will specify coding (using XHTML tags) that can identify features of indexes such as main entries and cross-references, it remains up to publishers to encode these features and up to reading systems to display them. Successful implementation of the standard therefore depends on its acceptance at each step of the production chain.

Sample coding (XHTML markup) can be seen at tinyurl.com/EPUBSample Markup. It's like reading a foreign language, but within this coding are index entries, locators, and cross-references, marked up with standard tags so that reading devices can manipulate them to create useful index displays.

The existence of standards is crucial for efficiency in ebook production. The inclusion of indexing in the EPUB standard will make it easier for publishers to provide indexes and for reading systems to display them effectively. A draft of the EPUB 3 index specification was approved by the IDPF board in March 2012. The draft was reviewed by IDPF members and other interested parties, and the Indexes Working Group has made its way through the suggestions and added new components including a schema. The revised specification will be reviewed again before its release.

Expert Tip

Indexing for reflowable text means that index entries have to be embedded in the text or linked to anchors within the text.

EBOOK INDEXING METHODS AND SOFTWARE

There are several methods of ebook indexing, mostly focused on indexing without page numbers.[15]

Methods

Tagging involves inserting a code or placeholder into the electronic text as a temporary locator. An example of this method is the Cambridge University Press (CUP) system, which requires the indexer to work from unpaginated documents in Microsoft Word format using temporary locators. These can later be used to generate page numbers for the index to a pbook or fixed format ebook. It may also work for reflowable ebooks.

Hyperlinking uses a markup language, such as HTML or XML (eXtensible Markup Language), to create anchors linking index entries to the text. Hyperlinking primarily occurs in website indexing, but can be used to create ebook indexes as well.

Embedded indexing means insertion of coded index entries into an electronic text file. Embedded indexes can be created in word processing or page layout programs and also in XML editors. Unfortunately, because each software module that generates indexes uses its own proprietary coding, many embedded indexing programs do not output hyperlinked indexes for ebooks, only page number-linked indexes for pbooks or fixed-format ebooks.

Numerous software tools exist to assist the indexer with linking, embedding, or hyperlinking. Many of them are designed to work alongside dedicated indexing software packages such as CINDEX, SKY Index, and MACREX. A set of scripts has been developed to assist indexers with InDesign-based ebooks (www.wright information.com/Indesign/Indesignscripts.html).

Software

Microsoft Word is a commonly used word processing program that offers some indexing features. Index entries can be embedded into the text using a unique tag and then hidden from view. Once entries have been embedded, the program can automatically generate an index with page numbers from the Word document. The index is usually not hyperlinked in PDF, rather only in Word, and it does not automatically translate to an ebook index. Further macros are needed to hyperlink the ebook index. There are several tutorials available to assist with using Word's indexing feature.[16]

Libre Office (download-libre-office.com) is a free office software suite that comes with a word processing package called Writer that supports a simple form of embedded indexing, similar to that offered by Microsoft Word. OpenOffice (www.openoffice.org) is a similar program with a shared origin.[17]

WordEmbed (jalamb.com/wordembed.html), an external embedding tool, can be used as an add-on for Word. Designed by Lamb, it is compatible with CINDEX, SKY Index, and MACREX. WordEmbed can assist with both linking and tagging, and has a specific feature for the CUP system. Again, once your embedded entries reside in Word, they do not automatically translate to an ebook linked index, and macros are needed to hyperlink an ebook index.

DexEmbed (www.editorium.com/dexembed.htm) is another external embedding tool that is used with Word for tagging or embedding. It is also compatible with CINDEX, SKY Index, and MACREX, and it can accommodate documents imported into layout programs such as QuarkXPress, Framemaker, and InDesign. DexEmbed can also assist with XML indexing using DocBook. As with WordEmbed, these embedded entries do not automatically translate to an ebook linked index.

InDesign is a popular desktop publishing program that includes an index creation feature. The biggest obstacle to use of InDesign for creating ebook indexes lies in the difficulty in transferring the indexing within the file into EPUB format. Wright and Olav Martin Kvern have produced a set of scripts for InDesign to help publishers get around this issue. Liz Castro has also developed a workaround and has written on creating an index for EPUB with InDesign and GREP.[18]

Online help authoring packages such as Madcap Flare (www.madcapsoftware. com/products/flare) and Author-it (www.author-it.com) have indexing modules that can create indexes for EPUB ebooks as well as for online help.[19] Indexes produced in Madcap Flare can link within topics, but for Author-it entries link to the top of a topic and use the topic heading as the text for the link. This works best when topics are not too long for easy scanning. Indexes can be manually created or derived from topic headings.

XML editors are increasingly being used to produce ebooks. Embedding tags into XML documents allows the generation of a page number or hyperlinked index. Michele Combs has written an excellent introduction to XML indexing techniques using examples from DocBook and DexEmbed. DocBook is one of a number of XML markup languages used to describe content.[20]

Expert Tip

Indexing for ebooks means thinking about how index entries will fit on a small screen and how indexes will be most usable in the digital environment.

EBOOK INDEX PRESENTATION AND STRUCTURE

To index effectively for ebooks, indexers will need indexing skills as well as awareness of the nature of the electronic medium and potential requirements for different standards and devices. There will be opportunities for expansion, such as the ability to use indexes and search functions together, and the use of structural information to refine index searches.

Indexing for ebooks requires a different workflow and a different approach to term selection and index structure. Software choice becomes important for linking or embedding indexes. Indexing will be influenced by the lack of page numbers, by the digital nature of the content (with similar issues to website indexing),[21] by the small size or variable size of the screen, and by new features in EPUB and other ebook specifications.

Suggestions follow, but these are options for consideration and are not intended for general application; in fact, sometimes contradictory alternatives are presented. There is no one-size-fits-all solution. Usability and accessibility should influence an indexer's decision making.

HOW TO INDEX FOR EBOOKS
Standard Approaches
While pbook indexers can assume a standard presentation of their index, ebook indexers will need to consider carefully how their index will appear and how the user will interact with the index. Ebooks can be read on devices with different size screens and can be viewed in different font sizes. Writing an index that is easy to use despite these variations can present a challenge. Many indexers have adapted their approaches from website indexing or online help indexing to ebook indexing. The following guidelines have been suggested:[22]

- Keep main headings and subheadings concise to avoid turnover lines on smaller screens. In cases where longer entries or sub-subheadings are necessary for the index, an intermediate-sized screen should be considered as the target.

- Keep the number of subheadings small so that they all display under the main heading on one screen and readers don't have to scroll too far through the index. Most main headings can be broken up into more precise terms. For example, information on cheese could be broken up into the main headings *cheese making*, *cheese microorganisms*, and *cheese varieties* rather than having these as subentries under the main entry *cheese*.

- Alternatively repeat main headings at every subheading, or, in a long list of subheadings, repeat the main heading concept as part of the subheading content here and there to remind readers of the main topic. For example, in a long section with *cheese* as a main heading, the indexer might occasionally include the word *cheese* in a subheading (e.g., *types of cheese*).

- Ensure that main headings and subheadings start with a keyword where possible (e.g., *usability guidelines* rather than *guidelines for usability*).

- Use one subheading per locator to avoid strings of undifferentiated locators. This removes the need for symbols or running numbers and avoids the problem of links at main headings being missed if there are also some subheadings.

- Use hyperlinked cross-references to guide readers within the index. Double-posting means that users don't have to follow cross-references, but it can result in duplicate hits if the index is searched.

- Use one column, without continued headings.

- Use group break navigation data/letter links/alpha bars (A, B, C, etc.).

- When structuring the index, think about the implications of outputting in different formats (e.g., print and ebook) or merging or splitting books. When merging or splitting, it is often good to have a subhead visible for each heading, even if it means that there will be orphaned subentries.

- Think about what the user will click on when using the index entries as clickable links (e.g., no page numbers, the text of the index entry is the link). If you have a main heading with a locator, and the main heading has subheadings as well, will the user click on the main heading or will they go to the subheadings first?

- Think about what you will use as the clickable link. When a book has no page numbers, the locator may be a paragraph or section number, a symbol such as an asterisk, or the text of the index entry. If you have linked from the text of a main entry as well as from subentries, will the user click on the main heading or will they go to the subheadings first?

New EPUB Approaches

The upcoming EPUB specification is expected to define coding that will expand the ways indexes can be used and the information they provide. Provision of more information about terms and their locators will allow users to filter the index to see just the parts they want.

While the EPUB specification has not yet been finalized, some aspects are likely to be implemented that will affect the way we index.

Concept Metadata

It is expected that EPUB will define coding (using XHTML tags) that allows publishers to provide concept metadata about terms (e.g., saying that they are flowers or mountains or names of authors). This could be used to:

- Expand generic cross-references. For example, if someone hovers over the cross-reference *prime ministers*, See also *names of specific prime ministers*, then all of the terms that had been tagged as *prime ministers* will be displayed.

- Filter the index. For example, the user could opt to show only *names of cited authors*, show *recipes* (e.g., in a book on healthy living), or show *foreign language terms* (e.g., in a scriptural index).

Locator Metadata

EPUB is also expected to define coding for the provision of metadata about locators (e.g., to say that the locator links to a table or a figure). This will show users what format to expect when they select a link and will enable filtering to show only locators leading to content in certain formats. Both content and locator metadata will be optional.

METADATA: COLLECTION-LEVEL, OPEN SOURCE EBOOK INDEXING

In addition to indexes, metadata is important for ebooks. Metadata has been described as data about data, and it includes information provided by booksellers and others to describe the books they are selling. It resembles library catalog information, giving details about subjects, formats, identifiers (e.g., ISBN numbers), and much more.

Metadata is crucial for the findability of ebooks, as shown in the Nielsen white paper on the link between metadata and sales.[23] EPUB ebooks must include title, identifier, and language along with the modified property (date the work was last changed) using the Dublin Core standard. ONIX for Books (www.editeur.org/83/ Overview), an XML-based standard for book metadata, can be included in EPUB 3 files. ONIX is used with Book Industry Communication (BIC) and Book Industry Standards and Communications (BISAC) subject codes from the U.K. and North America (and with other codes as required). There are plans to merge BIC with BISAC. These subject metadata codes are closely related to library subject headings.

Michael E. Bell's report on a NISO Ebook SIG webinar (tinyurl.com/ NISOebookSIG) noted that while ONIX metadata is considered best practice, some publishers would rather just capture the minimum information necessary for discovery of items. Publishers also noted problems mapping legacy systems that are based on MARC records and ISBN numbers to ONIX.

FUTURE OF EBOOKS

In the future, standard ebook indexes may be able to:

- Become part of the document structure, thus easy to find.

- Be displayed at the front or back of the book (with the potential to set the first-displayed page to jump past the index).

- Be accessed from any location in the text, allowing easy return to the place at which the user left the text.

- Be searched along with, or instead of, the text.

- Become active, linked to automatically or manually generated markers in the text, placed at individual words, paragraphs, sections, or pages.

- Become easily readable, with flexible formatting for device and user (e.g., having the option to collapse or expand main entries or letter groups).

- Provide information about the expected content in the text (e.g., while a pbook may show a page range, an ebook might highlight the targeted range of text or its background in a different color).

- Provide context for users browsing the index (e.g., using "tips" to show the main entry when a user hovers over a subentry).[24]

- Link to timed segments within audio and video files that are included in an ebook.

- Allow annotations by users (and authors and indexers) that would then supplement the index and provide ideas for indexers for the next edition.

- Provide mashups combining indexes to more than one work (e.g., an index of all the ebooks in a series or in a user's library).[25]

- Explore new options, like the visual index to *The Fry Chronicles: An Autobiography*.[26]

- Be provided in ebook samples, so that users can judge the book by its cover and its index.[27]

Once we have more ebook indexes in the marketplace, it will be interesting to perform usability testing to see whether people approach ebook indexes the same way that they use paper ones, to see how well traditional ideas translate to ebook indexes, and to explore extra features we may be able to offer.

What an exciting time to be an indexer! The work done by indexing advocates has ensured that indexes have been discussed in the technical, standards, and publishing communities. The views of indexers have been heard, and the vast experience of indexers has been recognized. In the next few years we will be able to build on this work and ensure the continuation of quality, active indexes into the future.

ACKNOWLEDGMENTS

While writing this chapter we were standing on the shoulders of giants. We would like to acknowledge the work done by many indexing society members and others to develop effective, appropriate solutions for the future of ebook indexing. In particular, credit goes to Jan Wright for her initiative, hard work, and deep understanding of indexing and software issues, and to Dave Ream and Michele Combs, the leads of the EPUB IWG. The ASI DTTF has also been helped by Michael E. Bell, Ina Gravitz, Mary Harper, Steve Ingle, Cheryl Landes, Joshua Tallent, Charlee Trantino, Pilar Wyman, and many others. From the Society of Indexers in the U.K., Bill Johncocks, James Lamb, and Maureen MacGlashan have contributed greatly to publications in this field; and in Australia, Mary Russell created the ANZSI webpage of ebook links.

ENDNOTES

1. DAISY (Digital Accessible Information System; www.daisy.org) is a technical standard that provides an audio substitute for print material. It was designed for use by people with print disabilities, such as blindness and dyslexia, and provides more sophisticated navigation and reading than a standard audio book.

2. Matt Garrish's ebook *What Is EPUB 3? An Introduction to the EPUB Specification for Multimedia Publishing* (O'Reilly Media, 2011) is a good introduction to the EPUB format and is available free as an ebook (shop.oreilly.com/product/0636920022442.do). See also Garrish's book *Accessible EPUB 3: Best Practices for Creating Universally Usable Content* (O'Reilly Media, 2011), also available free as an ebook (shop.oreilly.com/product/0636920025283.do#tab_03).

3. Simplified formatting guide for building Kindle F8 books can be found at kdp.amazon.com/self-publishing/help?topicId=A17W8UM0MMSQX6#back.

4. Jan Wright investigated the X-Ray function in the article "The Devil Is in the Details: Indexes versus Amazon's X-Ray" published in *The Indexer: The International Journal of Indexing* 30, no. 1 (2012): 11–16. This entire issue was guest edited by Wright. It can be purchased at www.lulu.com/shop/society-of-indexers/the-indexer-vol-30-no-1-march-2012/paperback/product-18952698.html.

5. For example, Mary Coe and Glenda Browne have considered this question in the following sources: Mary Coe, "The Tyranny of the Page," *The Indexer: The International Journal of Indexing* 30, no. 1 (2012): 2–5, www.lulu.com/shop/society-of-indexers/the-indexer-vol-30-no-1-march-2012/paperback/product-18952698.html; Glenda Browne, "Section and Paragraph Indexing," *The Indexer: The International Journal of Indexing* 30, no. 4 (2012), www.lulu.com/shop/society-of-indexers/the-indexer-vol-30-no-4-december-2012/paperback/product-20487163.html.

6. James Lamb's online article "Human or Computer Produced Indexes?" was updated in 2012 and can be found on the Society of Indexer's website (www.indexers.org.uk/index.php?id=%20463).

7. Peter Meyers offers many suggestions about ebook search at newkindofbook.com/
   2011/08/search-inside-ebooks-why-readers-look-what-they%E2%80%99re-finding.
   He also provides an excellent summary of why ebooks still need indexes at
   toc.oreilly.com/2011/09/ebook-index-search-discovery.html.

8. For more on this topic, see Wright's presentation "Indexing in Ebooks and Econtent:
   Adding Value" (www.toccon.com/toc2012/public/schedule/detail/21857) given at the
   2012 O'Reilly Tools of Change for Publishing Conference in New York.

9. For more on this topic, see Pierke Bosschieter, "The Kindle and the Indexer," *The
   Indexer: The International Journal of Indexing* 28, no. 3 (2010): 116–118.

10. A glossary and other content relating to ebook indexing are available at www.ptg-
    indexers.org.uk. One of the contributions of the Society of Indexers Publishing
    Technology Group to the IDPF Charter Proposal is at dl.dropbox.com/u/
    2248375/SI_Analytical_Index.pdf.

11. *Newcomers: A Selection of Articles for Those New to Indexing* (2012), edited by
    Maureen MacGlashan, is available in a Kindle edition (www.amazon.com/dp/
    B009YYZDI2) and as an EPUB (www.lulu.com/shop/society-of-indexers/newcomers-
    a-selection-of-articles-for-those-new-to-indexing/ebook/product-20482857.html).

12. Lamb's blog "… turning it off and on?" can be found at ccgi.jalamb.com/category/
    technology/e-books.

13. Dave Ream's "Anatomy of an EPUB Ebook" (www.asindexing.org/files/DTTF/
    Anatomy_of_ebook.pdf) provides a good introduction.

14. Documents from the Working Group, including minutes of meetings, are available at
    code.google.com/p/epub-revision/wiki/IndexesMainPage. The IDPF's EPUB 3 Indexes
    Charter can be found at idpf.org/charters/2012/indexes. See also Wright and Ream's
    "IDPF Index functionality in Epub" at dl.dropbox.com/u/2248375/IDPF%20Index%20
    functionality%20in%20ePub.pdf.

15. Bill Johncocks has examined issues relating to page-independent indexing and the use
    of embedded indexing, tagging, and hyperlinking in his article "New Technology and
    Public Perceptions," *The Indexer: The International Journal of Indexing* 30, no. 1
    (2012): 6–10, www.lulu.com/shop/society-of-indexers/the-indexer-vol-30-no-1-march-
    2012/paperback/product-18952698.html.

16. Wright has produced an excellent tutorial on indexing using Microsoft Word at
    www.wrightinformation.com/word.pdf. Peg Mauer also offers excellent advice in her
    article "Embedded Indexing," which appeared in *Key Words* (Jan./Feb. 1998 and
    Sept./Oct. 1998) and *The Indexer: The International Journal of Indexing* 22, no. 1
    (2000). It can also be found at www.edit-mb.com/embedWord.htm.

17. Information about conversion of OpenOffice to EPUB is available at www.pincette.biz/
    odftoepub/index.xhtml.

18. See the Adobe help page for creating an index at helpx.adobe.com/indesign/topics.
    html. Information Wright and Olav Martin Kvern's InDesign EPUB scripts can be
    found at www.wrightinformation.com/Indesign%20scripts/Indesignscripts.html. Liz
    Castro's blog on creating indexes for EPUB with InDesign and GREP can be found at
    www.pigs gourdsandwikis.com/search/label/indexes.

19. For more about Madcap Flare, listen to Cheryl Landes's webinar "Best Practices for Indexing Online Help" (www.madcapsoftware.com/demos/signup.aspx?id=11308688 57413419965). For more about Author-it, see www.seg-consult.com.

20. Michele Combs, "XML Indexing," *The Indexer: The International Journal of Indexing* 30, no. 1 (2012): 6–10, www.lulu.com/shop/society-of-indexers/the-indexer-vol-30-no-1-march-2012/paperback/product-18952698.html. As well, Dave Gardiner has written a book on XML in publishing, available for free at www.xmplar.biz/training.html#digpub with a linked index.

21. Issues to do with pageless indexing on websites, some of which apply to ebook indexes, were discussed in Glenda Browne and Jonathan Jermey, *Website Indexing: Enhancing Access to Information Within Websites* (Adelaide: Auslib Press, 2004), now available as a free PDF at webindexing.biz/website-indexing-2nd-edition.

22. These guidelines have been compiled from responses to a question on the Index-L mailing list by Wright, Cheryl Landes, and Maureen MacGlashan, and from Nancy Humphreys's five tips for making an ebook index at authormaps.com/make-an-ebook-index.

23. See Andre Breedt and David Walter's "White Paper: The Link Between Metadata and Sales" (2012), available at www.isbn.nielsenbook.co.uk/uploads/3971_Nielsen_Metadata_white_paper_A4(3).pdf.

24. You can see an example of "tips" in a website context in the Milan Jacovich detective series index at www.levtechinc.com/Milan/mjixb.htm.

25. A web-based version of a combined index to five books by Seth Godin can be seen at indexmasher.com/online/Linchpin-AllMarketers-PurpleCow-Tribes-Dip.html.

26. The iPhone app edition of *The Fry Chronicles: An Autobiography* can be found at www.itsbeenreal.co.uk/index.php?/new/myfry-iphone-app.

27. For more on use of indexes for book sales, see *Joe Wikert's Publishing 2020 Blog* entry "Rethinking samples" at jwikert.typepad.com/the_average_joe/2012/03/rethinking-samples.html.

Chapter 5

Indexing Literary Criticism

Martin White © 2014

Literary criticism is alive and well, quantitatively at any rate. Students in the early 21st century may be pursuing more market-oriented majors, but they are still taking English (and other language) literature classes. Universities are still producing English literature PhDs to teach those classes, and those new assistant professors are still publishing their tenure books to secure their places on the academic ladder. As a scholarly indexer (in which category I include the scholarly end of trade publishing), those books make up a significant part of my business. Of a total of about 650 book indexes I have done as of the date of this volume, 81 (or 12.5 percent) have been for *lit crit* titles, as I shall refer to them in this chapter.

Indexers who aren't scholarly specialists might hesitate to take on something in political theory, Islamic studies, or development economics; however, they might consider taking on a lit crit job because they took an English course or two in college, and it's just a big book report, isn't it, and how hard could that be? There is, perhaps, something to that line of reasoning, but the complexities and conundrums in lit crit indexing make it more challenging than indexing a mere big book report. I shall address some of those issues in this chapter.

WHAT IS LITERARY CRITICISM?

The *Encyclopædia Britannica* (15th edition) defines lit crit as follows:

> [A] discipline concerned with a range of enquiries about literature that have tended to fall into three broad categories: philosophical, descriptive, and evaluative. Criticism asks what literature is, what it does, and what it is worth.

These enquiries apply a wide variety of methods to a wide variety of genres of texts from a wide variety of critical perspectives. The method employed, the genre of texts studied, and the perspective of the author will all present particular challenges to the indexer.

VARIETY OF TEXTS

Lit crit texts do not follow one standard format. Some are devoted to a single author or even a single work of a single author. Others will be concerned with a school or group of authors. Yet others will focus on works from a particular region or historical period. Some will take as their subject works by authors that share a particular characteristic, such as women, people of color, or gays and lesbians. Others will focus on a principle or theme embodied in a broad range of works (e.g., advertising and commodity culture, authorship, the body, boredom, divine action, frontiers, nature, or 19th-century American clerks and office workers). And, as in other disciplines, there are multi-authored and "clean out the drawer" works.[1]

The nature of the text will very likely affect the sorts of problems that will confront the indexer. For example, a book on a single work or single author will delve deeply into a narrowly defined subject, likely resulting in long index arrays with many subheadings. The problem of indexing fictional characters in the works discussed (see the "Author-Title-Character" section later in the chapter) often arises in texts of this sort. Texts that cover a wider terrain often present many mentions of an author or work in disparate contexts that are sometimes difficult to organize into a coherent index entry. Multi-authored texts and "clean out the drawer" texts often contain chapters with widely diverse styles and approaches that are only tangentially related to the supposed subject of the book, making a consistent approach to the indexing practically impossible.

AUTHOR-TITLE-CHARACTER: HOW THE ELEMENTS FIT TOGETHER

There are three sorts of item that are almost universal in lit crit texts, at least those in which the works discussed come mainly from prose fiction. The first two, authors and titles of works, are, so far as the indexer is concerned, theoretically pretty straightforward. Authors are indexed by their surnames and titles of works are indexed as such. There are complications, of course: real names versus pen names, or multiple pen names. Titles may have both long and short versions (*The Adventures of Tom Sawyer* and *Tom Sawyer*). There are spelling and transliteration variants in names and titles. In an ideal world, volume and manuscript editors would regularize such discrepancies; in the real world of scholarly publishing, it falls to the indexer to sort them out in the index.

You must exercise discretion in indexing works of fiction. Attempting to trace turns of plot in the index entry can quickly get out of hand. I attempt to limit such indexing to general characterizations of the work, comparison to other works, and attributions of the author's general categories of analysis (e.g., race, class, gender, the body, colonialism, domesticity, modernism, nationalism, rationality) to the work. The following example is from Sara Guyer's *Romanticism after Auschwitz*:[2]

Frankenstein (Shelley)
   and apostrophe
   arms and hands in encounters between Victor and monster in
   as autobiography
   Coleridge's "Rime of the Ancient Mariner" and
   commitment to pass beyond the human in
   death penalty critiqued in
   discovery of origin of life in
   ending of; ethical function of
   failure of language in
   as figure for autobiography
   as frame narrative
   gap between first and second volume of
   human passions delineated in
   interruption in
   the Jura suggests ethical dimension of
   Levi's "The Survivor" and
   monster perceived as "figure of a man"
   monster's own narrative in
   mourning in
   and poetry
   preface to 1818 edition
   preservation of the human as aim of
   prognoses in
   and prosopopoeia
   romanticism's relationship to
   as self-reflexive
   Shelley's "Mutability" cited in
   as story of crisis of the human
   and testimony

Finally, in my experience, authors of lit crit texts are aware that index entries for the authors discussed and their works should be related in the index in some way, and they have often sought my assurance that I would indeed make such relationships (see "The Author Entry" section later in the chapter).

The third common entry type encountered in lit crit—fictional characters—seems to me to present particular difficulties for the indexer. These difficulties can become so intractable that I take a very minimalist approach to indexing them. If I can get away without including them in the index, in either main headings or subheadings, and still express the contents of the book, I do so. The principal ground for so indexing is that in most cases to attempt to index all of the mentions of a character's involvement in the various plot twists of a novel would require an effort of such magnitude that I cannot do it economically. In addition, from the qualitative point of view, trying to unravel the plot of a novel in index subheadings creates a problem that does not lend itself to elegant solutions.

Sometimes authors make it fairly easy to avoid indexing fictional characters. In those cases, an author will discuss a text principally in the context of general categories, such as those I have listed earlier, rather than in terms of character or plot. In such cases, those terms will comprise the bulk of the indexing in addition to author names and titles of works. Even in such cases, however, characters will sometimes be mentioned in a context such that the indexer sees no other way to index the passage without using a character name. While such cases are infrequent, I generally don't create a separate main entry for the character name, but use it only in a subheading. Further, I try to include some conceptual terms in the subheading to add context to the name and often, if grammatically possible, put the conceptual term in the filing position at the beginning of the sublevel. The following example is from Daniel Hack's *The Material Interests of the Victorian Novel*. You will notice that the alphabetization ignores forenames and terms of address:

Bleak House (Dickens)
    advertisements accompanying
    and Allsopp's Ale controversy
    on authority
    on authorship the marketplace and
    bodies as inscribed in
    Caddy's daughter's marks
    Caddy's inkiness
    dedication of
    Sir Leicester Dedlock
    Lady Dedlock recognizing handwriting
    Lady Dedlock's daughter
    dyer's hand image in
    Eliot's *Daniel Deronda* compared with
    Esther's illness
    Miss Flite
    handwriting in advertisements with
    handwriting's importance in
    Hawdon's letters
    Leigh Hunt and Skimpole
    Mrs. Jellyby dictating but never writing
    Jo at Nemo's inquest
    Krook's death

> Lewes's criticism of
> materiality of documents as concern of
> monthly numbers of
> Nemo
> Nemo's burial place
> and productive versus unproductive labor
> Shakespeare's Sonnet 111 quoted in preface to
> Skimpole
> on spontaneous human combustion
> synchronic organization of
> on text-body convergence
> Tulkinghorn's corpse
> Wragge of Collins's *No Name* compared with Skimpole

There are times, however, when the author's approach makes creating separate main index entries for principal characters unavoidable. I usually try to be as exhaustive as possible in my indexing (only once in more than 20 years of book indexing has a client complained that my index was too exhaustive), but when it comes to indexing fictional character names, as with titles, strict selectivity in indexing is my rule. Even in a short summary of a plot or episode, a character can appear in several contexts within a single paragraph or even sentence; the index entry could easily be overwhelmed with subentries mapping the character's path through the novel. To avoid this, I restrict my indexing to those contexts in which the author attributes defining characteristics to the character or in which the character embodies or represents the author's categories of analysis. When such entries are created, a *See also* cross-reference from the entry for the title to the entry for the character should be made. The following examples are from Keith Clark's *Black Manhood in James Baldwin, Ernest J. Gaines, and August Wilson*:

> *Fences* (Wilson)
> alternative models of subjectivity in
> array of black men in
> Jim Bono
> Cory
> countervoices in
> Lyons
> as male-dominated
> male-male conflict in
> on phallocentrism
> and re(en)gendering the black male dramatic subject
> Rose

sports and war as tropes in
See also Gabriel; Maxson, Troy
Gabriel (*Fences*)
   as assaulted on several fronts
   associational relationship to language of
   counterpatriarchal form of maleness of
   dance at end of the play
   institutionalization of
   on Lyons as "King of the Jungle"
   a rose for Rose
   as self-sufficient
   as spectacle character
   Troy's interactions with
   war experience of
Maxson, Troy (*Fences*)
   adultery of
   and baseball
   and the blues
   bluster of
   and Jim Bono
   and brother Gabriel
   death of
   and dominant fiction of masculinity
   incarceration of
   and Lyons
   maxims of
   as phallocentric
   shooting of
   and son Cory
   as storyteller
   and wife Rose
   women as orifices for

THE AUTHOR ENTRY

Index entries for authors can pose organizational problems. Such entries often grow quite large, and, as noted earlier, they need to be related to entries for the author's works. As paragraph-style indexes are the rule for scholarly books, and often for trade books as well, the result can produce a pretty unwieldy entry. A second level of subheadings can be a major improvement in such cases. Where paragraph style is required, the combined indented and paragraph style, with the editor's approval, can be used to impose some order on the chaos. Similar subheadings can be grouped together under an umbrella heading, including one for "works of" or "writings of." Following is a run-in example with sub-sublevels from Linda Furgerson Selzer's *Charles Johnson in Context*:

Johnson, Charles

> Buddhism of: articles in *Turning Wheel*; becomes more outspoken; on bodhisattva ideal; on Buddhism as refuge from white culture; deepening of; on mindfulness; on personal enlightenment versus social engagement; takes formal Buddhist vows; in tradition of originality; Zen Buddhism of

> as cartoonist: *Black Humor*; cartoon books of; "Give the Pig an Apple"; *Half-Past Nation Time*; "There'll Never Be Another Minister of Defense Like Malik"

> characteristics of work of: "black" aspect; Black Power and Black Arts movements' influence; black public intellectuals as subject; context of fiction; cosmopolitanism; eclecticism; history used as metaphor; intersubjectivity; intertextuality; philosophical studies influence fiction

> early life of; birth; high school education; sorority's cast-off books read by

> and King: conversion to King; engagement with King's legacy; meditations on King; views on King

> literary career of: awards; as book reviewer; critical studies of; Gardner as literary mentor; genealogy as black philosophical writer; goal in becoming a novelist; Northwestern University commencement address; philosophical fiction as chosen means of expression; as public intellectual; as University of Washington professor

> literary views of: on black philosophical fiction; on context in art; on Ellison; on fiction's capacity to change our lives; high-art aesthetic; on new black fiction; on whole sight

> personal characteristics of: journals and notebooks kept; martial arts practices; privileged background; son named after Malcolm X

> as philosophy student; as Black Studies program discussion leader; doctoral dissertation; doctoral studies at SUNY Stony Brook; doctorate awarded; economic difficulties during student days; engagement with Marxism; family's reaction to philosophy major; introduced to academic philosophy; leaves academic philosophy; Marcuse as interest; master's thesis; as neo-Marxist; philosophical evolution; philosophical interests; Reich's Marxist psychology as interest; Slaughter as influence; at Southern Illinois University; transition from Marxism to phenomenology; as trash hauler

political and philosophical views of: on class struggle; on one-sidedness of individual perspectives; on "scholars" versus "intellectuals"; on the sixties; on universals

views on race of: as "anti-race race man"; Black Power criticized; as child of integration; on suffering in black experience

writings of; "The American Milk Bottle"; "Be Peace Embodied"; "Blueprints of Freedom"; "Buddhism Is the Most Radical and Civilized Choice"; "China"; "Dr. King's Refrigerator"; "The Education of Mingo"; "Exchange Value"; "I Call Myself an Artist"; "The Katz Lecture"; "The King We Left Behind"; "The King We Need"; "A Lion at Pendleton"; "Mindfulness and the Beloved Community"; "The Phenomenology of the Black Body"; "Reading the Eightfold Path"; "The Role of the Black Intellectual at the Beginning of the Twenty-first Century"; "A Sangha by any Other Name"; "Searching for the Hidden Martin Luther King, Jr."; "The Second Front"; "Shall We Overcome?"; *The Sorcerer's Apprentice*; *Turning the Wheel*; "Where Fiction and Philosophy Meet"; "Whole Sight". *See also* "Alïthia"; *Being and Race*; *Dreamer*; *Faith and the Good Thing*; *Middle Passage*; *Oxherding Tale*; "Philosophy and Black Fiction"; "Wilhelm Reich and the Creation of a Marxist Psychology"

Note that the *writings of* subheading satisfies the condition of relating the author's name to his (in this case) works. When the entries for the works have only a few locators, and hence, no subheadings, I've double posted the title at this subheading. Where the entries for the works are analyzed, I've made a *See also* reference from this subheading as I did in this example.

POETRY

So far, I've mainly been discussing lit crit books that deal with prose fiction. Fiction represents the topic of perhaps 90 percent of lit crit books, but poetry and its analysis still remains a growing concern. For the indexer, there aren't many substantial differences between books discussing prose fiction and those discussing poetry. In both types of book, you'll encounter authors, titles of works, and analytical categories. Characters are less common in poetry, especially in the short poems that constitute the majority of modern poetry.

One difficulty that arises in poetry lit crit indexing more often than in fiction lit crit indexing comes from the fact that poems are typically published in collections. Thus, in addition to indexing the titles of individual poems, the titles of collections must also be indexed. As with relating authors and works, the index should show the relationship between the collections and the individual poems contained within them. Unfortunately, authors often neglect to make clear which individual poems reside in which collection. For example, when I was indexing Nana Wilson-Tagoe's *Historical Thought and Literary Representation in West Indian Literature,* I had to relate a number of poems by Derek Walcott to the collections in which they were published. Fortunately, I had access to a top-flight university library that held all of the works of Walcott. Lacking that, it might have been quite a task to procure that information. These days, the internet might offer sources of such information, although a 20-minute search of the web for the contents of Walcott's collections failed to yield them. For works in the public domain, the internet might be more useful.

This part–whole problem is not restricted to poetry, of course. The same sort of relationship pertains between short stories and the collections in which they are published and between individual songs and the albums that contain them.

BOOKS IN WHICH THE PRINCIPAL WORKS DISCUSSED ARE NOT ONLY FICTION OR WRITTEN

Scholars in recent times have cast their critical nets more widely than the traditional fiction and poetry texts. Kay Young's *Ordinary Pleasures: Couples, Conversation, and Comedy,* for example, discusses not only novels such as Leo Toltoy's *Anna Karenina* and Jane Austen's *Pride and Prejudice* but also television programs such as *I Love Lucy* and films such as Frank Capra's *It Happened One Night.* James Boyd White's *The Edge of Meaning* discusses Homer's *Iliad* and *Odyssey,* Plato's *Phaedrus,* poems by George Herbert and Robert Frost, paintings by Johannes Vermeer, Henry David Thoreau's *Walden,* and Mark Twain's *Huckleberry Finn.* Leah Knight's *Of Books and Botany in Early Modern England: Sixteenth-Century Plants and Print Culture* discusses early modern botany books and herbals. James Chandler's *An Archaeology of Sympathy: The Sentimental Mode in Literature and Cinema* discusses William Makepeace Thackeray's *A Sentimental Journey* and *Tristram Shandy,* fiction by Charles Dickens, the *Frankenstein* novel and films, and films by D. W. Griffith and Capra.

In such works, identical titles might occur for works in different genres. For example, in *An Archaeology of Sympathy,* there are three *Frankensteins,* a novel and two films. These had to be distinguished in the index by parenthetical glosses. Because throughout the index I was qualifying entries for works with the author's name, I couldn't simply fall back on (novel) and (film). Therefore, my entries were *Frankenstein* (Edison Studios), for the 1910 film for which the author names the studio but not the director; *Frankenstein* (Shelley), for Mary Shelley's novel; and *Frankenstein* (Whale), for the well-known 1931 film directed by James Whale.

This broadening of the scope of lit crit doesn't present any unique problems for the indexer. Authors, titles of works, and, sometimes, characters, as well as categories of analysis, occur in such nontraditional literary works. The indexer's general knowledge might be taxed a bit more by such works than by a text that discusses novels or poems only, but even the latter can assume such broad knowledge that the differences between traditional and nontraditional lit crit texts are negligible. There will be as much variation in difficulty within each category as across the categories.

WORKS THAT PRESUPPOSE SIGNIFICANT KNOWLEDGE OF A HISTORICAL PERIOD

Some lit crit texts focus very narrowly on works from a particular historical period (e.g., the 19th century, the Renaissance, the Romantic period, the Victorian era). Because the authors are usually writing for their professional colleagues, they often assume considerable background knowledge of the literary and historical context of the works that they're discussing. Unless the indexer is very lucky, he won't have this knowledge. This isn't unusual. Most of the time scholarly indexers are working on topics that fall outside their areas of expertise. Being a quick study is a requirement for the job. Some authors provide more of the background information, others provide less. In either case, the indexer will have to do some research in order to be able to create an accurate index. One benefit of having worked on a number of lit crit books is that over time the indexer begins to acquire some of the necessary background knowledge from previous jobs.

FOREIGN LANGUAGE LITERATURES

Just as the subjects of lit crit texts vary over historical periods, they also vary geographically and linguistically. By texts discussing foreign language literatures, I mean texts in English discussing works in French, German, Mandarin, Japanese, Spanish, and other languages. Sometimes, quotations in the original language are given in such texts, but the language of the text is English and all, or almost all, foreign language quotations are translated. Here again, while knowledge of the language at issue would be beneficial, most indexers are used to dealing with at least some material in languages other than their first language. It is a good idea to verify with the client that they are not expecting all foreign words in the index to be double posted for the original language as well as in English.

THEORY

Perhaps the principal difference between academic lit crit and book reports is that lit crit almost always has some sort of theory underlying it. Those theories have changed over time and academic fashion. Some of them are stated in reasonably straightforward language, others are so arcane as to be almost impenetrable to even the well-educated layperson. Among them are aestheticism, formalism, New Criticism, Marxism, historicism and New Historicism, structuralism, poststructuralism, postmodernism, and ecocriticism. Some of these terms will be index entries when authors of lit crit texts discuss the various critical approaches to the texts under their consideration.

Aestheticism ("the doctrine that art exists for the sake of its beauty alone, and that it need serve no political, didactic, or other purpose"), formalism (the view that "first, that form is the essence of art and, second, that form must be understood and therefore understandable [i.e., significant]"), New Criticism ("post–World War I school of Anglo-American literary critical theory that insisted on the intrinsic value of a work of art and focused attention on the individual work alone as an independent unit of meaning"), structuralism ("the school of thought …, in which cultures, viewed as systems, are analyzed in terms of the structural relations among their elements"), and Marxism are very much out of fashion in the early twenty-first century.

Historicism ("criticism in the light of historical evidence or based on the context in which a work was written, including facts about the author's life and the historical and social circumstances of the time"), poststructuralism (the view "that language is not a transparent medium that connects one directly with a 'truth' or 'reality' outside it but rather a structure or code, whose parts derive their meaning from their contrast with one another and not from any connection with an outside world"), postmodernism ("a late 20th-century movement characterized by broad skepticism, subjectivism, or relativism; a general suspicion of reason; and an acute sensitivity to the role of ideology in asserting and maintaining political and economic power"), deconstruction ("form of philosophical and literary analysis, derived mainly from work begun in the 1960s by the French philosopher Jacques Derrida, that questions the fundamental conceptual distinctions, or 'oppositions,' in Western philosophy through a close examination of the language and logic of philosophical and literary texts"),[3] feminism, and ecocriticism (which "address[es] the question, in all of its dimensions, how cultures construct and are in turn constructed by the non-human world")[4] are much more in fashion. These theoretical perspectives, especially poststructuralism, postmodernism, and deconstruction, tend to be much more jargon-laden and obscure than earlier critical theories. It is with them, also, that the much used, and perhaps abused, analytical trio of race, gender, and class most often occur. Indexing poststructuralist/postmodernist/deconstructionist lit crit can make for rough sledding and is probably not for the inexperienced indexer and certainly not for the faint of heart. For those interested in learning more to help when indexing this sort of critical approach, I would suggest Frank Lentricchia and Thomas McLaughlin's *Critical Terms for Literary Study*, 2nd edition, for which I indexed the new chapters.

WHAT IF I HAVEN'T READ THE BOOK?

You probably haven't. Even if you're a voracious reader, you'll have read only a small fraction of the number of texts analyzed in lit crit books that you might be asked to index. Competition is stiff in the study of Shakespeare, Austen, Dickens, and Proust; many young scholars seek to make their places in academia by studying lesser-known or neglected writers. In recent years, I've indexed books on Grace Metalious (yes, that Grace Metalious), Odysseus Elytis (1979 Nobel Prize for Literature), Jack Spicer (a minor poet associated with the San Francisco Renaissance), Hesba Stretton (a 19th-century writer of Christian children's books), and Edith Wharton (an important early 20th-century American novelist, now rather out of fashion). Like so much in book indexing, and certainly in scholarly indexing, you'll often be working outside of your area of expertise, or even your comfort zone. As someone whose personal reading is largely of nonfiction, I look at my lit crit indexing as a way to take those lit courses that I didn't have time for when I was an undergrad.

FILM, ART, AND MUSIC CRITICISM

As indicated previously, criticism has recently broadened its scope beyond the traditional written text. This development is correlated with a broadened theoretical understanding of the nature of a text, in which other entities, such as films, paintings, or pieces of music, can be "read" as texts. Many of the methods and theoretical orientations of lit crit have been applied to such objects. The upshot of this for the indexer is that if you can index lit crit, you can index film, art, and music criticism. You'll encounter authors (directors, painters, and musicians), titles of works, and sometimes characters. Many of the categories of analysis will be the same.

CONCLUSION

I hope that the foregoing has demonstrated that works of literary criticism are more than book reports. Indexing them presents both technical and substantive challenges. Are these challenges more daunting than those in other areas of scholarly indexing? Other things (the indexer's background, for example) being equal, I think not. Author-title-character relationships are no trickier than chronological relationships in history texts. Author entries present similar difficulties to entries for metatopics in other fields. All fields have their jargon, and most fields in the humanities and social sciences are theory-oriented, very often with the same postmodernist/poststructuralist/deconstructionist theory that is still common in lit crit. Any indexer who feels up to indexing texts in the humanities and social sciences should find lit crit indexing within his or her ability.

ENDNOTES

1. "Clean out the drawer" books are those in which the author collects several journal articles published at different times in different publications on somewhat related subjects and adds an introduction and a conclusion that attempt to frame them as a text on a unified theme.

2. While the published index appeared in run-in style, as is typical of scholarly indexes, I have used indented style here to make it easier to read the entries.

3. The definitions in the preceding sentences are from the online *Encyclopædia Britannica* (www.britannica.com), accessed October 11, 2013.

4. This is from the European Association for the Study of Literature, Culture, and Environment (www.easlce.eu/about-us/what-is-ecocriticism), accessed October 11, 2013.

REFERENCES

Chandler, James. *An Archaeology of Sympathy: The Sentimental Mode in Literature and Cinema*. Chicago: University of Chicago Press, 2013.

Clark, Keith. *Black Manhood in James Baldwin, Ernest J. Gaines, and August Wilson*. Chicago: University of Illinois Press, 2002.

Guyer, Sara. *Romanticism after Auschwitz*. Stanford, CA: Stanford University Press, 2007.

Hack, Daniel. *The Material Interests of the Victorian Novel*. Charlottesville, VA: University of Virginia Press, 2005.

Knight, Leah. *Of Books and Botany in Early Modern England: Sixteenth-Century Plants and Print Culture*. Burlington, VT: Ashgate, 2009.

Lentricchia, Frank, and Thomas McLaughlin. *Critical Terms for Literary Study*, 2nd edition. Chicago: University of Chicago Press, 1995.

Selzer, Linda Furgerson. *Charles Johnson in Context*. Amherst, MA: University of Massachusetts Press, 2009.

White, James Boyd. *The Edge of Meaning*. Chicago: University of Chicago Press, 2001.

Wilson-Tagoe, Nana. *Historical Thought and Literary Representation in West Indian Literature*. Gainesville, FL: University Press of Florida, 1998.

Young, Kay. *Ordinary Pleasures: Couples, Conversation, and Comedy*. Columbus, OH: Ohio State University Press, 2001.

Chapter 6

Let the Adventure Begin! Indexing Time-Spanning History Texts

Connie Binder © 2014

There is nothing like the thrill of receiving a history text to index—that sweet anticipation as you open the file, knowing that regardless of whether it is a scholarly tome, trade book, textbook, or government report, tales of marvelous adventure await. And imagine the potential delights and tragedies in a book that spans multiple decades or eons of time! Even the driest of them is filled with swashbuckling heroism and heartbreaking sagas of death and despair.

Time-spanning history books include general overviews of world history, surveys of a particular time period (Middle Ages), and investigations of a single topic (vampires) or place (Ireland) over time. Corporate or institutional histories are very popular for centennials and other anniversaries.

Providing readers with access to the grand adventures tucked away in time-spanning history books presents particular challenges to the indexer. We must create an index structure that includes all relevant access points, be faithful to the author's voice and argument, properly formulate entries for personal names and events that have been repeatedly named and renamed, deal with place names and political boundaries that change over time, and deftly handle the evolution of language so we can lead the modern reader to the past event. Because these books cover so much time and subject matter, it is important to make each index entry's scope clear. This requires more parenthetical glosses, as well as extensive cross-referencing, than might be used in other genres.

Fortunately, we have resources to aid us in our task. In addition to some very useful reference books and websites, the publisher's style sheet for the book can provide guidance for creating index entries, saving time for the indexer.

INDEX STRUCTURE

As tempting as it is to dive into the book and start indexing, you will save time and aggravation for yourself and the reader if you determine your index structure first. Whether your text spans decades or eons, time is an essential element in these books, and you must capture that in the index. Many of these books are organized chronologically, with each chapter representing a chunk of time. Others are organized geographically, or by topics, and flow chronologically within the chapter or topic. Expect to do a lot of double-posting. You want readers to find the information whether they look for it under a place, a time period, or a topic.

Time as a Main Entry

If the eras or time chunks have names (not just years), you can use these as main entries with topical and geographic subentries:

> Middle Ages
> > arts
> > England
> > France
> > religion
> > science
> Renaissance
> > arts
> > Florence
> > religion
> > science

Time as a Subentry

You may also want to include the time period as a subentry to places and topics:

> Churches
> > 5th century
> > 6th century
> > architecture
> > Byzantine Empire

If your eras are named, you can either intersperse these with topical subentries or add dates so they sort to the top of the alphabetical list of subentries:

Washington, D.C.
    Big Band era
    crime
    government and politics
    Jazz Age

or

Washington, D.C.
    1920s (Jazz Age)
    1930s (Big Band era)
    crime
    government and politics

Avoid having subentries that are just a year since these could be confused with page numbers. Try to add a parenthetical phrase or word that will separate the date from the page number:

Ferrari team
    1960 season
    1961 season

Combined Place/Time Main Entries

If the book is detailed and you are allowed only one subentry, you can avoid long strings of undifferentiated locators by adding era or timeframe glosses:

Asia (581–1100)
    arts
    class and society
    daily life
Asia (1644–1800)
    arts
    class and society
    daily life

Just be careful not to be too granular—you do not want to force the reader to look in too many places in the index. If there are only a few locators for each subentry under *Asia*, separating *Asia* by time period makes more work for the indexer and the reader.

Dynasties

Include named dynasties as main entries. If they are specific to a country, also include them as a subentry under the country. In the following example, *Abbasid dynasty* gets only a main heading post because it ruled a huge geographical area that shifted over the course of centuries, and for a time was a religious authority with no governmental powers:

> Abbasid dynasty
> China
>   Ming dynasty
>   Qin dynasty
>   Qing dynasty
> Ming dynasty (China)
> Qin dynasty (China)
> Qing dynasty (China)

AUTHOR'S VOICE AND ARGUMENT

In addition to the time periods, places, and events, you have to make sure that your index provides access to the metatopic of the book. Kate Mertes gives a wonderful talk "On Aboutness," in which she makes the point that the metatopic acts as more than just a topic; it is the author's argument—his slant on history. The introductory chapter often provides an outline of the book so you can see how the author's argument will be supported through time or events in each chapter.

In discussions with an author of a book about the Sacco and Vanzetti case, which spanned several decades of American history, the author made it clear that World War I, the draft, patriotism, anti-immigrant sentiment, the labor movement, and anarchism were not only important historical items, but the combined effect of them played a pivotal role in the convictions. Knowing this before beginning made it easy to pick up and properly situate references to the events. These formed main entries as well as subentries for Sacco, Vanzetti, and their trials:

> anarchism and anarchists
>   immigration restrictions on
>   in Sacco-Vanzetti trial
>   World War I
> draft, military
>   evasion
>   exemptions
>   in Sacco-Vanzetti trial

    Sacco-Vanzetti trial
       anarchism testimony
       draft evasion testimony

Author's Slant in the Language in the Index

The language you use in the index will reflect the author's argument. Corporate histories are often written for anniversary celebrations and tend to display the company in a very positive light, glossing over racism, sexism, labor violence, and other unflattering aspects of their history. Skull-splitting union-bashing may be hidden within the text of the book under the guise of labor relations. You need to use the terminology and tone from the book, but allow access for readers who may be looking under a term different from the author's:

    Labor relations
       discordant
       harmonious
    Unions. *See* Labor relations

NAMES

Princesses! Rascals! Philosophers! Thieves! History contains an endless cast of fascinating characters to index. These characters also present one of the greatest challenges to the indexer. You may encounter one person referred to by many different names, different people referred to by the same name, one-word names, and rulers and royalty. You need to bring together all references for one person under one main entry, with cross-references from other forms of the name. And you need to make sure not to combine two different people into one index entry. In addition to sorting out who is who, you will need to determine the appropriate initial element of the name for the index entry to sort on.

There are guidelines, there are principles, there are general practices that specific groups of people in specific places generally followed most of the time. Except when they didn't. If you are indexing people from a place or time other than your own, you must look them up in a reference source to verify their names for indexing. It can be incredibly time-consuming, but it saves you the embarrassment of later realizing you have created an index with separate, non-identical index entries for the same person, with no cross-reference, because you had no idea these were the same person. Your research will also confirm the initial element of the index entry for sorting. This is painstaking, nit-picky work. You may occasionally need to remind yourself of how fascinating these characters are as you spend hours of time figuring out their proper name.

Reference Sources for Names

Start your search with *Merriam-Webster's Biographical Dictionary*. It only covers the deceased (my edition dated 1995 means people deceased prior to that year), but it provides entry order for multi-part names, cross-references to alternate names, and a brief biography of each person. Use the spelling and form of the name that is used in the text, with the entry order from the dictionary.

If the author's form of the name is not the form preferred by the biographical dictionary, make a cross-reference from the *Dictionary*'s preferred usage. For example, if the text talks about *Tah-gah-jute*, and you look in *Webster's*, you will find a *See* reference leading you to *Logan, James*. Your index entry will reflect the text, with a cross-reference from *Webster's* preferred form:

> Logan, James. *See* Tah-gah-jute
> Tah-gah-jute (Mingo leader)

This is beneficial to readers who most likely are more familiar with the standard dictionary version of the name and will look for it that way in the index. Another benefit the index provides occurs when the text uses two (or more) versions of the name, without any mention that they are the same person. This happens often in a text with multiple authors. By having the cross-reference in the index from the first encounter with the person, you will know that you have met the same person upon your next encounter. In these situations, bring the entries together under the name used most prominently, and alert the editor about the discrepancy in the text.

For living people and others not listed in *Webster's*, you can check the Library of Congress (LOC) Name Authority files. There is a trick to using LOC Authority Files. Like a good index, it includes extensive cross-references. If an entry in the list is labeled *References*, it is a cross-reference, not the preferred entry order for the name. Click on the link to find the *Authorized Heading*. If you click all the way into the record, you want the name as it appears in the 100 field. Use the LOC authorities for determining the entry element of the name, but take your spelling cues from the text.

When you cannot locate a name in a reference source, an excellent guide for determining the entry element and format for the name is *Indexing Names*, edited by Noeline Bridge. It provides guidelines for names from different time periods and places.

After all of your diligence, if you are still unsure about a name, make the index entry that makes the most sense and label it in your indexing software. Sometimes these will be clarified later in the text. If not, you can send a list of the questionable entries to the editor for double checking.

One Person With Multiple Names

History is a series of wonderful stories. As these stories are recounted, names are translated, transliterated, mangled, and misunderstood. Over the course of years and places, one person may become known by a number of different names. As indexers, we need to bring together all of the information about one person under one index entry, with cross-references from other forms of the name that the reader may search under.

Sometimes the author will knowingly use more than one name for a person, first introducing the variants ("Avicenna, also known as Ibn Sina"), and then using either name interchangeably. In this case, choose one form as the main entry, including the alternate as a parenthetical gloss:

> Avicenna. *See* Ibn Sina
> Ibn Sina (Avicenna)

The gloss enables the reader to locate the information on the page of text, regardless of which name the author has used in that particular place.

Different People With the Same or Similar Name

As you index, you may come across a name that you have picked up earlier in the book. Realize that this may not be the same person. If the previous reference was in a different era, place, or topic, verify whether this is the same person, especially if it is a common name. When you have multiple people with the same name, you will need to give readers enough information so that they can determine which one they are looking for. Provide a parenthetical gloss that gives distinguishing information about date of birth, profession, or whatever is appropriate for the text:

> Gaius (Roman general)
> Gaius (Caligula), Emperor (Roman Empire)
> Gaius Octavian. *See* Augustus, Emperor (Roman Empire)
>
> Holmes, Oliver Wendell (b. 1809)
> Holmes, Oliver Wendell (b. 1841)
>
> Ibrahim Lodi, Sultan of Delhi
> Ibrahim the Crazy, Ottoman Sultan

If you are adding a title, put it in parentheses at the end of the entry so that names read alphabetically:

Smith, George
Smith, John (Capt.)
Smith, John (Rev.)
Smith, Michael

It may read more poetically to enter a title and name in direct order and force sort them, but this nonalphabetic format can be confusing to readers and some publishers forbid it:

Smith, George
Smith, Capt. John
Smith, Rev. John
Smith, Michael

One-Word Names

One-word names were not invented by 20th-century pop stars. You will encounter many historical figures who, in their own day, were every bit as famous as Madonna. Because readers may be less familiar with Fidelis than they are with Bono, add a parenthetical gloss to one-word names. In addition to giving clarification to the reader, it will assist you in editing the index. You will know that Mosco is a person, not a typo:

Abawayh (Abbasid potter)
Iakovlev (Cossack captain)
Mosco (Powhatan interpreter)
Nana (Chiricahua Apache)
Tecumseh (Shawnee leader)
Xenocrates (Greek philosopher)

Royalty

To distinguish these titled figures from one another, you must include the name, title, realm, and possibly dates and nicknames. I have seen a few different style options for including all of this information. Check the publisher's style sheet to see if they have a preferred format. If not, pick one and apply it consistently throughout the index:

Charles X, King (France)
or
Charles X, King of France
or
Charles X, King of France (1824–1830)

In her chapter of *Indexing Specialties: History*, Sandy Topping suggests adding dates to the main entry for royalty. For large books with characters who appear repeatedly in different chapters, this can be quite helpful to the reader and the indexer.

Imagine you have successfully struggled through the names of all of the kings of France and you move on to the chapter on England. There you encounter "Charles, the king of France." Your index contains ten French kings named Charles. You can curse the author's vagueness, go back to the text, reread all of the Charles references, double-check with *Webster's* for dates and additional information to figure out which Charles this might be. Or if you have done a little more up-front work by adding the dates of reign to the index entries, you can just navigate to *Charles* in your index and by comparing dates, quickly determine which Charles ventured to England. Adding the dates creates more work in the initial entry but can ultimately save a lot of time and frustration. For publishers whose style omits the dates, I have sometimes included the dates as I index so I can keep the characters straight, and then deleted the dates before sending the index to the client.

Nicknames and Translated Names

Some people are best known by a nickname, for example, "William the Conqueror" or "Charles the Bald." Spanish kings may be "Carlos" in Spain, but referred to as "Charles" in other nations. Take your cue from the text for the main entry and add cross-references from other forms of the name. Be aware that more than one person may share the same nickname. Incorporate the nickname into the main entry so readers know when they have found the person they are looking for:

> Charles II (the Bald), Holy Roman Emperor
> William I (the Conqueror), King of England
>
> Barbarossa. *See* Frederick I (Barbarossa), Holy Roman Emperor; Khayr
>   al-Din (Barbarossa)
> Frederick I (Barbarossa), Holy Roman Emperor
> Khayr al-Din (Barbarossa)
>
> Carlos III, King of Spain. *See* Charles III, King of Spain
> Charles III (Carlos III), King of Spain
>
> Catherine, Duchess of Cambridge
> Kate, Princess. *See* Catherine, Duchess of Cambridge
> Middleton, Kate. *See* Catherine, Duchess of Cambridge

Cross-References for Foreign and Familiar Names

In your research, you will have determined the initial element of the name for sorting in the index. You will also need to provide cross-references from alternate entry elements under which the reader might reasonably search. This becomes particularly important when dealing with people from different countries and eras of history. In addition to foreign names with multiple parts, you will encounter historical figures that readers are familiar with, but refer to by names other than the initial index entry element.

Foreign Names

For multi-part last names, provide cross-references from the element of the name that isn't the initial entry element. This isn't always necessary with Spanish or Portuguese names, but include any form under which you think a reader might reasonably search:

> Garcia Márquez, Gabriel
> Márquez, Gabriel Garcia. *See* Garcia Márquez, Gabriel

Historical Names the Modern Reader "Knows"

Readers know to look under the last name of a person to find the index entry. For some historical figures, the last name that is used in popular culture may be different from the name that reference sources would have us use. You will want to provide access for both the casual reader who is familiar with the popular form of the name and for the scholar who is accustomed to searching under the "official" form of the name. Use the form of the name that the author uses and provide a cross-reference from other entry elements:

> Bonaparte, Napoleon. *See* Napoleon I, Emperor of France
> da Vinci, Leonardo. *See* Leonardo da Vinci
> de Gaulle, Charles. *See* Gaulle, Charles de
> Gaulle, Charles de
> Leonardo da Vinci
> Napoleon I, Emperor of France

INSTITUTIONS

Institutional or corporate names present challenges similar to those of personal names. You will deal with name changes and alternate names for one institution, multiple different institutions bearing the same or similar names, and you will need to determine the appropriate entry element. Included in this category are ships, companies, museums, government entities, universities, and other institutions.

One Institution, Two Names

You would think that an institution would be solid and unchanging. Ha! The big decision is whether it is appropriate to put all of the information under one main entry with a *See* reference from other forms of the name, or if it is better to put each instance under the name at the time, with *See also* references between the two. This will depend on the nature of the text.

Keeping Both (or All) Forms as Entry Points

When there are clear differences between the two names and the author maintains the distinction, keeping the index entries separate with a *See also* link is the most appropriate:

> A.C. Cruise Lines. *See also later name* Boston Seaport Boat Charters
> Boston Seaport Boat Charters. *See also former name* A.C. Cruise Lines
>
> Amelia Occasions. *See also later name* Historic Venues, Inc.
> Historic Venues, Inc. *See also former name* Amelia Occasions

Choosing One Name as the Entry Point

Sometimes an author will introduce an institution as "the Boston Marine Society, also known as the Friendship Club," and then proceed to use the two names interchangeably. Because these are the same entity, you will want to choose one as the main entry and create a *See* cross-reference from the other. In order for readers to locate the information on the page, you will need to add any alternate forms to the index entry as a parenthetical gloss:

> Boston Marine Society (Friendship Club)
> Friendship Club. *See* Boston Marine Society

Without the parenthetical gloss, someone who looks up *Boston Marine Society* might get to the page of text and not find it; the only reference on the page may be the Friendship Club.

When an institution name appears in translation, it is not uncommon for the author to use multiple forms of the name, transposing words in different instances in the text. Choose one and make cross-references from other forms of the name:

Military History Museum (Moscow)
Moscow Military History Museum. *See* Military History Museum

Ships, Aircraft, Vehicles, and Vessels

Enter ships under the actual name of the ship, not initials such as USS, RMS, or
HMS that precede the name. The ship name should be italicized. If they appear in
the text, add the corresponding initials (USS, RMS, HMS, etc.) to the index entry
in Roman type after the name of the ship. For ships without leading initials, add a
parenthetical gloss to denote the type of ship:

> *Great Britain II* (ketch)
> *Irwin*, USS
> *Kearny*, USS
> *Titanic*, RMS

If a ship name is composed of a person's name, do not invert it:

> *E.A. Johnson* (sloop)
> *James E. Kyes*, USS

If a ship has a common nickname, add that as a cross-reference:

> *Constitution*, USS
> *Old Ironsides*. See *Constitution*, USS

Names of vehicles and vessels should be italicized, with a parenthetical gloss
denoting the type of vehicle:

> *Discovery* (space shuttle)
> *Hindenburg* (dirigible)
> *Spirit of St. Louis* (airplane)

Makes, models, and generic classes of vehicles are not italicized. Add a parenthetical gloss when needed to clarify the index entry:

> Ford Mustang
> Porsche 911 RSR
> Spitfires (fighter planes)

PLACE NAMES

In a history text confined to a certain time period, place names may be relatively stable and not cause you much anguish. But properly locating and naming places in a swashbuckling multi-era history book can be daunting. Political boundaries change; countries get divided, combined, and renamed; areas may be in dispute, claimed and named by different nations. Preferred transliteration schemes change, creating new spellings of words from other alphabets. Because modern readers may not have a thorough knowledge of geographic history, you also need to provide access from the current name of a place to the name used in the text.

When in doubt, *Merriam-Webster's Geographical Dictionary* will give the history of a place as well as previous names and alternate names and spellings. *Indexing Names* has a "Geographic Names" chapter that provides excellent guidance.

Physical Features

There is an important distinction between physical geographical features (rivers, lakes, mountains) and political entities (Soviet Union, Mexico, New York). A mountain may be named differently by different peoples, but it is the same mountain. Unless the author makes cultural distinctions requiring separate entries, choose the form most prevalent in the text and make a cross-reference from any others:

> Ayers Rock. *See* Uluru
> Uluru (Ayers Rock)

I recommend that you invert the feature type if it is the leading element, so the name is the initial element of your index entry. Add a cross reference to get readers from the generic to the specific:

> Everest, Mount
> Gulf ___. *See specific gulf by name*
> Lake ___. *See specific lake by name*
> Mexico, Gulf of
> Michigan, Lake
> Mount ___. *See specific mount by name*

If space allows, double post entries directly:

> Everest, Mount
> Gulf of Mexico
> Lake Michigan

> Mexico, Gulf of
> Michigan, Lake
> Mount Everest

Political Entities

Name Changes During the Course of the Text

Political entities are much messier to deal with. Often a place name changes due to political events. Even if the boundaries remain the same, the nature of the place may be different enough that different main entries are warranted. The distinctions between pre-revolutionary Russia, the Soviet Union, and the Russian Federation after the collapse of the USSR probably require making these separate main entries. If the author does not use terms interchangeably, neither should the indexer:

> Djibouti. *See also former name* French Somaliland
> French Somaliland. *See also later name* Djibouti

Name Change After the Timeframe of the Text

The text you are indexing may entirely take place before a country's name changed. For instance, if the text only deals with the colonial era and does not mention the post-independence name of a country, you will need to index it under the name used in the text, with a *See* reference from the current name so that modern readers can find what they are looking for:

> Bangladesh. *See* East Pakistan
> East Pakistan

> Djibouti. S*ee* French Somaliland
> French Somaliland (Djibouti)

Variant Forms of Political Entities

Choose the primary one used in the text and make a *See* cross-reference from the other(s):

> Soviet Union
> Union of Soviet Socialist Republics. *See* Soviet Union

Britain/British Empire/British Isles/England/Great Britain/United Kingdom

The British (or is it the English?) provide us with great adventures in indexing, not the least of which is deciding how to index their motherland. There are historical and geographical differences in the various terms, described in great detail in

Merriam-Webster's Geographical Dictionary. Within a given text, an author may use any or all of them. You need to determine if the author is making an actual distinction between different entities or is just trying to mix things up for better readability. If there is an actual distinction, index these places as they appear in the text and make *See also* cross-references between them. When two or more terms are used interchangeably, choose one and make *See* cross-references from the others. I find *Webster's* extremely helpful for figuring it all out. It provides a history of the various jurisdictions, including the geographic areas they included at specific points in time.

Nationality vs. Nation

Because entries for the nationality of a people may not sort near the country name, make cross-references as necessary:

> France. *See also* French diet and cuisine
> Great Britain. *See also* British diet and cuisine

TERMINOLOGY

Language evolves. Words are coined, become obsolete, and take on new meanings. Your task is to get modern readers using modern language to past events which may be described in unfamiliar (though charming) terms.

Newly Coined Phrases

Every day, inventions are created, scientific processes are developed, and acts of glorious heroism and villainy are performed. It may take years before their significance earns them a name that sticks. There is a long list of discoveries that were discussed in the literature before having a name. Examples include Alzheimer's disease, Halley's comet, and Higgs boson. This is tricky for the indexer, and relies somewhat on one's knowledge of history. Be alert when indexing eye-witness accounts and historical documents. If you know the modern name for what is described, use it.

Obsolete and Unfamiliar Terms

Enchanting as it may be, historical terminology may be unfamiliar to the reader. Add a parenthetical gloss to clarify obsolete or uncommon terms in the index. Readers may have a vague idea of what something was called and be able to get close to the correct place in the index. With the gloss, they will know when they have reached the correct index entry. This also allows for serendipitous finds that spark a reader's interest:

chonhado (wheel map)
cimora (psychotropic drink)
cladding (cookware process)

Racist and Other Offensive Terms

Eyewitness accounts and historical documents may contain racial epithets, derogatory terminology for people with mental illness, and other language that offends the modern reader.

If a book on African American history includes terms such as *colored men*, *negroes*, *Blacks*, and *African Americans*, gather them all under the modern term. Make a cross-reference from any versions readers may look under:

> African Americans
> Black Americans. *See* African Americans

For organizations and named movements and events, use the proper name, even if it includes obsolete terminology; these are the actual names and you cannot alter them:

> Black Arts Movement
> Colored American Institute
> Negro Convention Movement

EVENTS

Events are what make history so exciting—battles, fires, floods, sit-ins, and marches! Tales of triumph and disaster, heroism and devastation! You will need to situate the event in time and space, differentiate between multiple events with the same name, and bring together all references to one event that is so incredible that it has been called a number of different things.

Time Gloss

For all events, whether straightforward or difficult to tease out, add the year in a parenthetical gloss. For books that span nations as well as time, a country qualifier may be appropriate. The detail necessary will vary depending on how much time and space your text covers:

> Auspicious Incident (1826)
> Self-Strengthening Movement (19th-century China)

Battles

For battles, lead with the location of the battle, and include the year(s). Add a generic cross-reference to direct readers:

> Alcazar, Battle of (1578)
> Battles. *See specific battle locations*
> Stones River, Battle of (1862–1863)
> Trenton, Battle of (1777)

One Event, Different Names

Make a main entry using the event name that the author uses most often, with a cross-reference from any other term(s) that the author uses or that you think readers may look under:

> Boston Molasses Disaster. *See* Great Molasses Flood
> Great Molasses Flood (1919)
>
> Great War. *See* World War I
> World War I
>
> Chicago World's Fair. *See* World's Columbian Exposition
> World's Columbian Exposition (Chicago, 1893)
>
> Corps of Discovery Expedition
> Lewis and Clark Expedition. *See* Corps of Discovery Expedition

Different Events, Same Name

For different events that happen to have the same name, add a parenthetical gloss to differentiate them:

> Five Year Plan (Argentina, 1947–1951)
> Five Year Plan (Argentina, 1951–1955)
> Five Year Plan (Soviet Union, 1928–1933)
>
> "great retreat" (1915)
> "great retreat" (1930s)

PUBLISHER'S STYLE GUIDELINES

Many publishers supply specific styles for their books, and write style sheets in an effort to maintain consistency. For indexing, there may be a general indexing style sheet that covers the formatting applicable for all of their book indexes. In addition, there is often an editorial style sheet for each specific book. You may have to ask for these.

Indexing Style Guide

This will let you know the publisher's formatting preferences to set in your indexing software for main entry style, cross-reference style, italicization, punctuation, and how to treat illustrations, tables, and figures. It may also let you know if the publisher has a preference for formatting entries for place names and royalty:

> Charles I, King (Great Britain)
>
> or
>
> Charles I, King of Great Britain

> Laurel, Maryland
>
> or
>
> Laurel, Md.
>
> or
>
> Laurel (Md.)
>
> or
>
> Laurel (Maryland)

Style Guide for the Book

Publishers often put together a style sheet for the editorial team working on a book. This can be a gold mine of information and save you a lot of work looking up names and trying to determine if two potential index entries are actually the same entity.

The style sheet may include the list of reference works used by the author and editors; a list of personal names in index-entry order; a list of place names; or a list of terms with preferred spelling, capitalization, and hyphenation. It may have the preferred term to use for the first occurrence of a word, with acceptable second-use terminology. This can be very helpful; for example, when you encounter "the ring," you will know that it belongs with your index entry for *Nürburgring race course*.

CONCLUSION

The care and detail required to properly index a time-spanning history text are significant. It is no small feat to create a solid index structure, echo the author's voice, and keep straight all of the names, places, and events.

As with any difficult endeavor, the rewards are also great. The adventure of indexing a history text gives us the opportunity to live vicariously through the exploits of the heroes and villains, become more connected with human foibles, and relive favorite stories from the past. But the greatest reward is knowing that we have provided readers with an efficient portal into history, enabling them to quickly find the daredevil or escapade they seek.

REFERENCES AND FURTHER READING

Bridge, Noeline, ed. *Indexing Names*. Medford, NJ: Information Today, Inc., 2012 – Buy this book. Among other things, it covers the general problems with names, names by nationality or ethnicity, names by genre of text, and clearly explains how to use the Library of Congress Authority Files. It is a phenomenal resource. Buy it now.

The Chicago Manual of Style. 16th ed. Chicago: University of Chicago Press, 2010 – The indexing chapter is absolutely amazing. It covers personal names and place names as well as providing a wealth of indexing information. This is a recognized authority within the publishing world.

Library of Congress Authority Files. authorities.loc.gov (accessed October 11, 2013) – These can be very helpful for determining the appropriate entry element for a name. *Indexing Names* has a chapter devoted to understanding how to use the authority files.

Merriam-Webster's Biographical Dictionary. Springfield, MA: Merriam-Webster, 1995 – This is my go-to place for looking up personal names. It has brief biographies and extensive cross-references. It only includes dead people.

Merriam-Webster's Collegiate Dictionary. 11th ed. Springfield, MA: Merriam-Webster, 2008 – Great for helping to understand outdated terminology.

Merriam-Webster's Geographical Dictionary. 3rd ed. Springfield, MA: Merriam-Webster, 1997 – Explains physical and political place names, with history. This will clear up any questions you have concerning similar names, and different names for the same place.

Mulvany, Nancy C. *Indexing Books*. 2nd ed. Chicago: University of Chicago Press, 2005 – Includes a chapter devoted to names, covering personal names, geographic names, and organization names.

Perlman, Janet, and Enid L. Zafran, eds. *Index It Right! Advice from the Experts, Volume 2*. Medford, NJ: Information Today, Inc., 2010 – Deborah Patton's chapter on indexing military/naval books is particularly useful for indexing history books.

Towery, Margie, ed. *Indexing Specialties: History*. Medford, NJ: Information Today, Inc., 1998 – Great information on indexing history in general, with chapters on specific eras and types of texts.

Chapter 7

Indexing Scholarly Books Across Cultures

Celeste Newbrough © 2014

Globalism is an irrepressible force driving academic and nonfiction publishing. Today, the need to understand other cultures and peoples, their history, economy, and social conditions is a prerequisite of good education. Indexers are by definition interested in the human condition and in the open-ended discovery of what is common across humanity and what varies. Since understanding our world is of necessity a cross-cultural effort, regional and cultural studies are fertile ground for contemporary thought.

When I first attended university in the 1960s, I managed to plough through German and Spanish. The influence of Europe on my own hemisphere was a sufficient factor to take into account in my education. However, the emergence of Asian economies, especially the economies of the two population giants, India and China, has resulted in a new turn eastward. The early 20th-century philosophical preoccupation of the West with Eastern culture is now conjoined with a canny interest in material survival, for these economies will continue to greatly impact our own.

Today, in some cases, Chinese is taught at the grammar school level and studies in Chinese, Russian, Indian, and Japanese cultures are common in secondary education. Essential to a broad education in the 21st century is some understanding of the cultures, economies, and histories of nations in the European Union, Asian cultures like India, Korea, China, Japan, and Indonesia as well as Africa, the Americas, and other world populations.

As a scholarly indexer, I work primarily on such international and regional works as well as studies of subcultures within the United States. I am often confronted with books that look at a single country or culture, synthesizing history and sociopolitical analysis around a topical inquiry such as politics, the status of women, or an aspect of the economy. Other multicultural texts move in the opposite direction, examining sweeping implications of a sociopolitical or historical trend across cultures, or comparing nations regarding a specific measure such as democratic values or economic competitiveness. Books about the history of science, the environment, or technology construct narratives of a cross-cultural and pan-historical nature. All such texts cross-contextualize place to theme and from theme to place producing a complex and often nonlinear structure of information. The richness of these books must be mined by the indexer with both thoroughness and austerity.

My involvement with regional and cultural books began with work on subjects such as ecology, comparative economics, or religious studies. Having worked on some studies of the history of religion, I attracted the interest of a major Buddhist scholar, Robert E. Buswell at the UCLA Center for Buddhist Studies, who translated Asian mystics. Thus I was thrown into the world of diacritics and ancient wisdom of the East. Gradually more secular Asian works came my way, so that Asian-related regional studies, then Latin-American regional studies came to form a significant part of my indexing.

INDEXING MULTICULTURALISM

Multicultural analyses include both regional national studies and examinations of subcultures within a country. Looking back again to my experiences as a student in the 1960s, subcultural studies were rare and not focused on in academic curricula in the U.S. Not until the 1970s did authors of African-American history and culture, or women's studies, struggle for publication and acceptance in departmental curricula. Following these groundbreakers, other cultural analyses came to the fore exploring the Latino/Latina experience, Jewish-American and Asian-American cultures, and onward.

It's amazing what you can learn reading academic texts today. Recently, I indexed two scholarly works featuring the historical and cultural role of hip hop music. In a larger work on incarceration of African Americans, a University of Notre Dame team of scholars explored the iconography of hip hop and rap, its relation to the prison culture, and how commercial co-optation of hip hop encouraged the elements that many now find offensive, such as sexist and violent references. Another book looked at hip hop from the perspective of the Puerto Rican-American community, Puerto Rican contributions to hip hop, and how this participation impacted the community itself. Encountering these texts in which history, cultural artifacts, and sociopolitical analysis are enmeshed, it is important to include all important topics but to construct them in such a way that the reader who is interested in a given topic can be satisfied without having to wade through confusing and extraneous information. Through cross-references, the reader is informed of the wider implications and interaction of that subject, which can be discovered.

Regional and transnational analyses typically involve tracing transnational historic forces and the spread of cultural artifacts both ideological and material. At the time I encountered Jack Goldstone's *Revolutions and Rebellions in the Early Modern Era*, I was in my early phase as an indexer. I found the profusion and fusion of information daunting, as every chapter seemed filled with multiple levels of analysis. Understanding the structural relationships between these schema of information is a challenge to the indexer, because without relating these multiple tiers of facts, it is impossible to understand what to index in the book. But attempting to explicate these relationships in the index can result in over-complicatedness. An index does not explain the contents of a book; rather, it provides a guide to those contents. Goldstone explored the use of weaponry, a rather minor topic compared to others such as class structures and power hierarchies. I could have indexed the details of this rather limited topic of invention and style of weaponry, first by each nation, then under that nation by each weapon, its type and style, history of development, political impact, and so on, resulting in an overly complicated and repetitive index. Within that country entry, the details of weaponry would have competed with far more wide-reaching topics related to class relations of the structure of power.

Instead, I structured the index to focus on these themes in a more general way by country and elaborated on the details within a topical listing. An example of the first, ineffective approach would be:

Qing Dynasty: complaints of the peasantry; gunpowder; canons history and use; militarism; peerage system and ranking of nobility; pistols invention and use; rifles; use of weapons as a means of control

And then repeating such a polyglot for every artifact of culture along with themes of analysis within every country discussed like, the *United States (canons; rifles; pistols; class subtopics; political subtopics; geographical subtopics; France: all of the above; Great Britain, Ottoman Empire, Japanese Shogunates, Moghul Empire)*.

Another way of dealing with the multiple layers of information is to break them out into discrete topics:

Qing dynasty: history and use of weaponry (*See also* weaponry); peerage system and ranking of nobility, etc.
American revolution, impact of canons on (*See also* canons; weaponry)
governments' use of weaponry
gunpowder: invention of; proliferation to Western countries; use by Qing Dynasty
weaponry: canons; pistols; rifles. *See also* gunpowder

The reader of a multicultural text who is interested in the Qing dynasty would then be guided to important entries like *history and use of weaponry* and *peerage system and ranking of nobility*, rather than having to plow through a plethora of subheads related to different topics.

I have struggled greatly with such issues of over-complicatedness in this and other books, often finding such efforts time-consuming and bringing down my earnings per hour, since like most indexers I charge by the page. I've learned in 20-plus years as an indexer to readily analyze information into structural blocks that I can deal with in a more simplified fashion, using cross-references when needed to show the reader the transnational implications of a topic.

CROSS-CULTURAL ANALYSIS

I find that the multicultural books that cross my desk cover various specific subjects, yet the texts cover a common ground of material applying it to a given region, culture, or cultural topic. I cannot count how often I have indexed topical references from Michel Foucault, among the founders of the postmodernist approach. Whether the topic is history of science and technology, regional studies, philosophy, or a social science, what my editors and authors send to me are complex analyses of social analyses. Postmodern social theory is the common thread uniting the multicultural body of work.

Working with books related to different cultures steeps the indexer into a cross-cultural perspective. Cross-cultural studies are greatly stimulating and satisfying to me. While I traveled more extensively when young, my current journeys challenge me to unravel the consciousness of other countries and languages.

Most works of social theory link historical forces with current events. The processual and temporal elements of real events is difficult to capture in an index. For this reason, I try to include aspects of the text focusing on temporality and change or transformation.

Class analysis and economic factors are also important to emphasize in the index. An unspoken premise of most social theory is that the world of ideas is grounded in the material world. Social theorists are critical thinkers. Seldom does a work of theory present only one perspective, rather the author offers several approaches and using factual arguments and reason, comes down on the side of one of these. The index cannot reflect the wholeness of an author's argument; however, it is important to point to what is unique in the narratives and convergences of each work.

The ideas of great modernists are still influential in works of social theory. Due to space constraints, I can only list those who occur often in my texts: Theodor Adorno, Martin Heidegger, Hannah Arendt, Henri Bergson, Edmund Husserl, Antonio Gramsci, Karl Marx, and even the largely unscientific intuitions of Sigmund Freud.

However, as I touched upon earlier, contemporary regional studies are often more infused with leading postmodern thinkers and ideas. Postmodernism as a strategy of historical and cultural analysis does not propose or favor one ideology or "truth" above another, but evaluates the authenticity or facticity of a social idea in multiple contexts, showing how diverse factors shaped its development. While the modernist boldly ventured into generalizations both superb and untenable, the postmodernist does not avail herself or himself of such luxury. The tools provided by thinkers like Foucault, Jacques Lacan, Luce Irigary, Jacques Derrida, Gilles Deleuze, Judith Butler, Julia Kristeva, Homi Bhaba, and others enable contemporary scholars to carefully differentiate between opinion and fact, between generalization and actual hypothesis. Through meaningful discussions of such authors occurring in the works I have indexed, I have been led to explore directly the ideas of these theorists. While social science is not pure science, today's well-written study sets up arguments that future authors can specifically address and refute.

A recent book I worked on by physical anthropologist Kimberly Tallbear titled *Native American DNA* combines science with cultural and racial analysis. This engrossing work spans from genetic science to the author's personal odyssey as a Native American academic. Like other cultural analysts, she based her text in postmodern analysis and racial formation theory. I needed to index her facts with headings like *blood quantum rules* and then add extensive targeted and topical subheads. I also focused on her ideas; for example, I included the following:

> author's perspectives: as an anthropologist and Native American; on blood talk and DNA talk; on cultural hybridity; on gender and communication style; on genetic composition and tribal membership; as a participant observer of genetic genealogist postings (see Rootsweb.com study); on personal tribal lineage; on traditional knowledge

Her opinions and conclusions about the impact of genetic tests on Native American populations also needed to be captured in the index headings similar to *genealogical and scientific critiques of.*

MULTICULTURAL ANALYSIS WITHIN THE BROADER FIELD OF SCHOLARLY INDEXING

With every new encounter with a scholarly manuscript, I have learned something new not only about the subject but about the composition of an index. I would describe the main task of scholarly indexing as to identify the thematic tiers of the book, which might include cultural, economic, religious, linguistic, and other themes. Once understanding the structure of the work, the indexer's task is to produce *the simplest and most usable index*, using terms that as much as possible emerge right out of the text. This way it is easy for the reader to find that topic on the page. At the same time, other listings by which the reader might look for the topic must also be in the index.

The more linear a work is, the more readily an indexer can sail through it. But some books require additional effort, and a good indexer is willing to bite the bullet sometimes. Each book calls for its own treatment and must be given the time and energy needed to compose a usable guide.

I recently indexed a book on the ancient Orthodox church at Asinou, in Cyprus. Over centuries, layers of murals were applied by various artists in different periods, then eclipsed by later works. The authors weaved together artistic, religious, historical, regional, and scientific perspectives (analysis of paints and materials, etc.) on the art of this small church designated as a World Heritage Site. I did not know initially that the multiple authors and editors spent over 39 years compiling the book. I was assigned the task of indexing it in one month. While the book was a work of surpassing scholarship, it lacked certain features that a book of its kind needed, for example, a separate catalog of works, an extensive map, and a plan of the church. In addition, the various authors placed emphasis on different aspects of the art, history, and religious symbolism. Making sense of this multiplicity of information was an arduous mission. But the visual splendor of the book made my "charitable" contribution worthwhile. A year after my effort I received a copy of this splendid book, a work of art in and of itself, making my sacrifice more palatable.

It is precisely the complexity of structure that differentiates a scholarly work from others. A scholarly work is not linear, thus a simple analysis of content is inadequate to provide a guide to the content. The qualities of a scholarly indexer are the same as that of any scholar: a questioning and analytical mind; a knowledgeable background; and the commitment to do what is required to bring a work to completion meeting the standards of publication.

Scholarly texts generally proceed with multiple analytical structures. The author(s) might bring to bear the history, culture, and political economy of a nation or region, and sometimes a specific theoretical perspective to address a topic. For example, a recent scholarly work I indexed related to the status of women in India. The work, by outstanding Indian-Australian anthropologist Kalpana Ram, examined the various theoretical and practical ways in which public service workers categorized the "problems" of women of the lower castes in rural India. Reformulating the ideas of philosophers ranging from Michel Foucault to Maurice Merlou-Ponty, and examining the history, caste situations, and religious experiences of these women, Ram constructed an extraordinary defense of the integrity of these women and their coping skills. The inescapable conclusion of her book is that health and psychological services must be more responsive, rather than attempting to reach public policy goals with a set of one-size-fits-all bureaucratic interventions. The complexity of an important book of this kind is confounding even to the best of indexers. Yet the reward of intimately participating in the book by compiling the index is equally great.

Scholarly indexing differs from general nonfiction indexing (such as trade book indexing) in several ways. I don't mean to put down general nonfiction. For example, Randy Shiltz's nonfiction book on the AIDS epidemic, *And the Band Played On*, is a book that contains some of the most high-value information one could find, yet it is a journalistic rather than a scholarly work and would be much simpler to index. The information is presented in a dramatic way ensuring a wide readership, and it is essentially laid out in narrative form. Most scholarly works are intended to impress other scholars rather than to expand popular readership. They are seldom simple narratives but are complex expositions of tiered information. The indexer is challenged to present topics related to multiple themes in a simple and elegant manner. This is a major challenge.

The challenges are manifold to an indexer of multicultural and international works. Indexing books across cultures and regions involves several areas of specialty: first, a firm grasp of the principles of indexing and specifically of scholarly indexing; second, an interest and background in other cultures; third, a theoretical grounding in contemporary social thought; and fourth, experience and technical skills.

THE WORK OF AN INDEXER

In conclusion, I would like to share insights gained from my experience as an indexer. There is a huge misunderstanding on the part of even some editors, but certainly the general public, of what an indexer does. It is a difficult field, especially since, if you are one of those who have the skills and intelligence to produce a good index, you are likely to have entered another field that gains greater income and prestige. I can understand why, for there is no way really to teach this skill, only to forewarn and encourage.

As a student or researcher, the reader approaches a work in a certain way, underlining ideas or facts that he believes are important and that he will need to learn and remember. But the indexer's approach is quite different. Instead of figuring out what the author means, the indexer determines what is of meaning (in other words, what information is contained) in the text, and how the reader can best access this information. This is a slight but profound shift in practicum. The work of the indexer is not explication but the location and structuring of information. An index is not an abstractly balanced outline of a work, it is a collaborative effort married to the language and meaning of the book.

The indexer's goal is to ensure that a book reaches its widest relevant audience. The indexer needs to create a structure that is adequate to guide the reader to each level of analysis. Simplicity and complexity together must always characterize the indexer's approach. The indexer must avoid at all costs the error of over-complicatedness. If historical, cultural, economic, and theoretical themes cluster around the factual matter of the book, the indexer cannot get lost in explicating these relationships through her or his work. The indexer asks certain questions and on that basis formulates an approach to the book: What narrative or narratives is the author telling? Who is the book written for? Who will be the typical readers and what sort of interests will cause them to encounter this book and its content?

The most important task of the indexer is to differentiate foreground from background. Without doing that, the indexer cannot produce much better than a concordance. A concordance is a simple, often digitally produced list of every mention of a name or phrase. Concordances are the worst sort of indexes, serving at best for a highly technical work that constitutes its own entity without referring to the real world and containing no narrative, theory, or opinion. The reader is presented with a string of page numbers and no clue as to what is important and what is not. It is the task of the indexer to guide the reader to important information contained in the book. No more, no less.

The indexer needs to think diligently about how a reader will seek information and ensure as much as possible that the reader will find what he or she is looking for. Essential functions are cross-referencing and double posting important entries as well as understanding the relationships between concepts and facts: which are identical or similar, which are contained within another, and which are related and which are not. Even in the absence of such in-depth knowledge of a subject, a good indexer can take his or her clues from the text itself. When confronted with the unknown, the text must serve as the guide.

As every rule must have its exception, sometimes the subject of a paragraph or section is not found within it at all. St. Augustine's famous spiritual autobiography, *Confessions*, includes several pages of lines similar to this: "I fled Him, down the nights and down the days; I fled Him, down the arches of the years; I fled Him, down the labyrinthine ways." Nowhere on these pages appears a word or term that denotes the subject of this poetic section, a man's relationship with God.

If a book is poorly structured or unbalanced, the indexer must decide whether to impose a more rigid structure or to reflect the book in its own intuitive construction. This latter approach might be best if the index is to become a real usable guide to the contents. A book on the history of the petroleum industry, going back to my first decade as an indexer, was hugely problematic in that the text was saturated with various layers and kinds of information but very poorly written, poorly structured, and poorly edited. In such cases, the indexer must face what everyone else has been able to pass on—a work that is essentially a failure. The indexer does have the potential to serve as the book's redeemer by actually extracting what is essential and presenting it in a coherent way. But in most cases, the indexer fails, as did the author(s) and editor(s) all along the line.

The techniques of indexing are signatures of each indexer. Ideally, how one approaches the work depends on the work itself; however, one must encounter a new work with some preexisting set of techniques and technologies. Some index-ers merely scan but do not read a book. They must be brighter than I am. I read the book. To read means to examine each sentence, paragraph, and chapter and to understand what information it contains. I read the book in its entirety, or by chap-ter or section, either before or in tandem with inputting of the index. If a book is really challenging, such as a work I will undertake this spring on the philosophy of science, I still prefer to work with the hard copy. Though it takes more time, I'm more confident of the final product.

My efforts with Asian diacritics and other foreign words and letters has been rewarded by the new and surprising meanings revealed in another language, words, and ideas unfamiliar and untranslatable in English. The discovery of such new words, phrases, and meanings is to me one of the rewards of cross-cultural schol-arly indexing.

To me, the work of an indexer is enormously gratifying though sometimes tinged with loneliness and angst. I feel fortunate to have stumbled into the rare and largely misunderstood field of scholarly indexing. The indexer's mind must be at once wide-reaching and detail-oriented, a difficult state to attain. The abilities of each indexer evolve with each project. As I proceed in my third decade of work, issues I used to struggle with in composing an index now come naturally. During my first decade as an indexer, I expended enormous energy learning the craft and wound up poorly paid for my time. But something about the work caused me to continue to tell myself, "This is my work and no one else's."

Indexing is a craft that above all is self-learned. I have been asked to rescue indexes that someone else finally threw up their hands over and gave up on. I could readily have done that several times in my early efforts. But not giving up is the key to becoming a master indexer, just as it is the key to success in scholarship and sci-ence. Charles Darwin once famously claimed, "It's doggedness that does it!" So don't give up.

Chapter 8

Medical and Science Indexing

Anne-Marie Downey © 2014

A lifetime ago, I embarked on a career as a journalist. Fired up by post-Watergate fervor to discover and report the truth, I studied, trained, and eventually worked in both the broadcast and print media. I interviewed the senator who conducted the hearings that led to the downfall of an American president. I found myself in a locker room filled with NBA prospects who only wanted to strip off their sweaty uniforms and head to the showers. I covered the tragic story of a mother who sought to kill her young daughter and then commit suicide but only succeeded in drowning her child. But most days the details of local government—budgets, zoning, and petty politics—absorbed my attention. In all my endeavors, I sought to gather and process information and then to present that information in the manner most appealing and accessible to the listener or reader. As publisher Henry R. Luce said:

> Journalism is the art of collecting varying kinds of information (commonly called "news") which a few people possess and of transmitting it to a much larger number of people who are supposed to desire to share it.

Years passed and life intervened in accordance to the wisdom of John Lennon. I found myself casting about for work that would allow me to continue to seek knowledge, wield words, and share information. Happenstance and fortune in the form of a newspaper article about a flourishing firm that filled an intriguing niche in the publishing world led me to indexing. My experience in reporting and writing and the requisite computer skills secured an on-the-spot tryout with my mentor. So overdressed for the interview (I did not yet know indexers practically invented casual Friday … and Monday and so on) and unfamiliar with the software, I called upon all my preparation to that point. I took hold of the pages and began to do what I had always done: find information and help the reader. But these particular pages contained material unlike any I had handled before. I would not be indexing history or politics or any general topic that I might have encountered as a journalist. My mentor's specialty was medical indexing, and the projects that she potentially would be sending my way would come from that field. I relied on the fearlessness

I had needed as a journalist and perhaps a touch of the arrogance, too. As writer Dave Barry said, "We journalists make it a point to know very little about an extremely wide variety of topics; this is how we stay objective." I doubt that first effort at medical indexing produced any exceptional entries, but my mentor detected sufficient potential to give me the opportunity to become an indexer.

In the decade and half since, I have created hundreds of indexes. For many years, I worked almost exclusively as a medical indexer. But as the publishing industry has evolved, contracted, and gone global, I have expanded my repertoire to include various topics in the hard sciences such as biology, botany, and chemistry while still retaining a special interest in anatomy and physiology, medicine, and pharmacy/pharmaceuticals. I have discovered that many indexers shy away from these fields. While their reluctance to delve into this material may be good for my business, I believe most indexers possess the skills necessary to create clear and credible hard-science indexes.

Perhaps my less-than-traditional path to indexing has given me a unique outlook. The task of the journalist is to conquer complicated facts, figures, and expert accounts and to transform the information into articles or stories that the reader can grasp and utilize. How different is that really from the job of the indexer? Publisher Joseph Pulitzer's description of journalism could serve as a mission statement for indexing as well:

> Put it before them briefly so they will read it, clearly so they will appreciate it, picturesquely so they will remember it and, above all, accurately so they will be guided by its light.

Indexing is a means of imparting essential information. The hallmarks of both my journalism and indexing careers have focused on the gleaning and presentation of information. I do not display the personal habits that I understand many indexers share. My spices are not alphabetized, and my closet doors barely close. I have always contended that a messy desk and a tidy mind are not incompatible. The organization of information—not my household—is my bailiwick. I have mastered the art of hard-science indexing to the extent that I have by trusting in the lessons I learned in Journalism 101. When indexing, I employ the tried-and-true basic questions of news writing: the 5Ws + H. Focusing on these questions of Who, What, When, Where, Why, and How could help other indexers gain the confidence and competence to venture into science and medicine.

WHO

With the reader's needs as the principal concern, the indexer first must answer the question of *who*. Science texts serve various populations of readers: science and medical professionals, college students, and everyday people seeking to educate themselves about their health and their world. The level of detail and complexity in an index should be dictated by the characteristics of the readers. Generally, the publisher provides this information, or the preface or introduction may provide it. Above all else, the indexer strives to meet the needs of the reader. Indexers must constantly step back from the material and regain the perspective of the reader. The difficulty of high-level science and medical texts can sometimes consume the indexer who then produces insular indexes that fail as guides for the reader. Guard against this by asking yourself if you would understand the index if you were a reader new to the material. Of course, your entries should reflect whether the reader is a student struggling with the subject or a physician or scientist seeking to expand his or her knowledge. Similar material should be presented differently, depending on the background and goals of the reader. For instance, I created entries on antibodies in three different books.

In a basic book for phlebotomists, I kept the information concise and simple:

Antibodies, 80–81
   in blood types, 121–124, 122*f*
   production of, 117
   transport in blood, 109

In a more advanced college biology text, I generated greater detail with the expectation that the reader would be seeking more information:

Antibodies, 148, 304, 352, 748, 1069
   and agglutination, 1080, 1080*f*
   binding sites of, 1072–1074, 1074*f*
   diversity of, 1074–1075
   gene recombination hypothesis for, 1075, 1075*f,* 1076*f*
   HIV and, 748–749
   in humoral response, 1080, 1081*f*
   production of, 1071, 1078–1079
   regulatory sequences and, 352–354
   selective adhesion of, 148–150, 149*f*
   specificity of, 1069, 1071, 1074–1075

In the highest level text, a book on nuclear imaging, the entries became even more realized:

Antibodies, radiolabeled or monoclonal
 anatomy and physiology review for, 112–113
 crossfire effect of, 112
 diagnostic use of, 25*t,* 112–114
 imaging/therapy with, 112–117
 nomenclature for, 24*t*
 production of, 112
 therapeutic use of, 25*t,* 112–113, 114–116

While the reader is the only one with whom I would be concerned in a perfect world, the realities of the publishing industry require that authors also receive attention. Occasionally, I find the requests and submissions of authors to include beneficial information that clarifies the language and structure of the index. More often I must work to balance the suggestions—dare I say whims—of the writers with the compelling interests of the reader. The profession of indexing mystifies many authors, and their closeness to the material can cloud their judgment. The "indexes" and suggestions I receive from writers usually are concordances that include incidental information and unworkable entries such as stand-alone adjectives. If the indexer submits an accurate, comprehensive, and readable index, the author often realizes that is the preferable approach. In cooperation with the editor or project manager, I do my best to incorporate the author's wishes while still remaining true to a commitment to the reader and the indexing profession. I use the author's lists or requests as guidelines and check my entries against them to ensure that no critical material has been omitted.

WHAT

With the material posing unique challenges, the indexer next must address the question of *what*. Subject matter in the science and medical text can intimidate even seasoned indexers. When I tackle a new topic or even return to material after a long interval, I often feel a moment of panic, asking *What have I gotten myself into?* But experience has taught me to take a deep breath and to begin slowly and deliberately. Whenever possible (when the pages do not arrive in separate batches), I try to reflect on the text as a whole and form a general approach for the index. Front-of-the-book material can provide crucial context. The table of contents can pinpoint the general topics; the preface or outline can elucidate the goals of the text. Within the body of text, science books often provide guideposts or clues. Like many textbooks, these texts usually employ section headings. The indexer must be careful not to rely solely on these for content and wording, but they usually offer worthwhile considerations. Terms in boldface or italics nearly always indicate material to be indexed. Other textual clues are less obvious. The readouts for figures and tables sometimes condense and clarify the main ideas and may be helpful to the indexer seeking to create succinct and accurate entries. Chapters of science and medical texts often conclude with notes or references. These also can make the language and content clearer.

Beyond the text itself, the indexer can consult many resources. The indexer must exercise all the recommended cautions when seeking information on the internet, but the web offers an amazing array of information sources: dictionary definitions, the periodic table of elements, and even scholarly articles that can provide explanations of advanced concepts. Sometimes just seeing the content expressed in different language can make the idea click. Useful reference books include *Stedman's Medical Dictionary*, *Physicians' Desk Reference*, and specialized dictionaries for the individual disciplines of biology, botany, chemistry, and other hard sciences. Indexers also should build their own library of indexes. This library should include your own indexes, indexes from previous editions of texts, and samples of indexes you discover through your browsing or reading. These indexes can provide valuable inspiration and even reveal approaches that can resolve your indexing dilemmas. Mentors or networks of peers also may furnish guidance and recommendations.

The science and medical indexer must always remember that expertise in the field is the responsibility of the author. The indexer's job is to "translate" the material and to provide lucid and efficient access to the text. Much like the journalist, the indexer must possess an open and keen mind. Television anchor Diane Sawyer described the critical characteristic of both reporters and indexers: "If you're curious, you'll probably be a good journalist because we follow our curiosity like cats."

WHEN

With the task of creating entries at hand, the indexer must confront the question of *when*. Indexers sometimes falter when faced with the complexity of material in hard-science texts and fail to adhere to the basic tenets they follow in all other areas of indexing. Sound and sane decision making still must be applied, which means the indexer determines when material merits inclusion in the index. The indexer must be able to disregard mentions that merely would serve as distractions from the substantive discussions. Newcomers to medical and science indexing find these choices difficult and stressful since so much terminology looks important. Before adding page references to your entries, question whether the reader would find the information at that location truly useful. We are creating indexes, not concordances. The indexer cannot permit the unfamiliar or challenging vocabulary to distort or overrule professional judgment. Indexers have strongly developed senses of when to index—the key is to trust those instincts. Author's notes, listings of key terms, glossaries, and previous indexes can confirm the indexer's choices, but the indexer remains the professional arbiter.

Other issues of when include setting a maximum number of page references, determining when to break entries into varying levels of subentries, and indexing material in figures and tables. The main entry should only include page references to the general or most substantive material regarding that topic. The number of page references should not exceed five to eight just as in any other good index. I prefer limiting the string of page references to five or six whenever possible within space constraints. Subentries should be employed to differentiate page references and to add more specific, helpful information for the reader. For instance, in my index for a pediatric pharmacotherapy text, I delineated the information for cellulitis in addition to offering a general page range:

cellulitis, 608–10
    clinical presentation of, 609
    diagnosis of, 609
    microbiologic etiology of, 609
    periorbital and orbital, 616–618
        clinical presentation of, 616–617, 617f
        diagnosis of, 617
        microbiologic etiology of, 616
        predisposing factors for, 616
        treatment of, 617–618, 632t
    treatment of, 609–610, 630t

In the same index, I used subentries to avoid a lengthy list of stand-alone page references for the drug azithromycin:

azithromycin
    adverse effects of, 552
    for cryptosporidiosis, 572
    for cystic fibrosis, 227
    for group B *Streptococcus* prophylaxis, 505
    for otitis media, acute, 534
    pediatric dosing of, 563t
    for pertussis, 552, 553t
    for pharyngitis, 540
    for pneumonia caused by atypical organisms, 560–61
    for sickle cell disease, 791
    for traveler's diarrhea, 578
    for *Ureaplasma* infection, 502

The indexer should review any entry that goes below a third level. A fourth level rarely may be advisable if it is permitted by the client, but it should always be scrutinized for a better approach. Material in figures or tables often augments the information in science and medical texts. Given free range or specific instructions, I mark these page references with italic *f's* or *t's,* but guidelines sometimes require plain-face designations as in the previous examples. Some publishers also request that these special indications not be employed, and I then determine whether the figures or tables are included in the existing page range for the entries or if an additional page reference (even without the *f* or *t*) would be helpful to the reader.

WHERE

With the goal of crafting an index thrifty in words but rich in reader experience, the indexer must confront the question of *where.* The structure of the index determines the ease of access for the reader. Indexers can create convoluted indexes that lead readers into dense thickets of meaningless words, or they can fashion clean, clear indexes that guide the reader through the text. Decisions on where indexers place information—determining what should stand as main entries, adding subentries for clarity and description, and selection of cross-references—draw the map for the reader. Indexers sometimes become ensnared in the technical nature of medical and science texts and feel compelled to include too much information in one location. My first indexing mentor warned me about this "outline" approach and reminded me that our purpose was not to pile all the information at one location but to give the reader numerous access points to the text. Indexers do not replicate the text; indexers make the text manageable and accessible.

Topics in science and medical indexing often have to be broken down into numerous main entries. Relying on a single main entry would generate the dreaded outline approach and do little to serve the needs of the reader. I generally employ the adjective and noun structure for multiple main entries. Consider these entries from an anatomy and physiology index. I have included only the main entries:

Abdomen
Abdominal aorta
Abdominal aortic plexus
Abdominal aponeurosis
Abdominal cavity
Abdominal muscles, in respiration
Abdominal nerve plexuses
Abdominal oblique muscle

Abdominal region
Abdominal thrusts
Abdominal wall, muscles of

Only the general entries are included in the main *Abdomen* entry. Further description and information is given in the various *Abdominal* entries. I used a similar approach for a geology text. Again, only the main entries are shown:

volcanic ash
volcanic eruptions
volcanic gases
volcanic glass
volcanic hazards
volcanic island arc
volcanic landforms
volcanic landslides
volcanic mudflows
volcanoes
Volcanoes National Park (Hawaii)

Finally, from a chemistry text:

Electron(s)
Electron affinity (EA)
Electron capture
Electron configurations
Electron delocalization
Electron geometry
Electron groups
Electron pair acceptor, acid as
Electron pair donor, base as
Electron sea model
Electron spin

Please note the use of (s) with the *Electron* entries. When using the adjective and noun structure, I use this to force the most general entry to the top alphabetically. Burying *Electrons* between *Electron pair donor, base as* and *Electron sea model* would be a disservice to the reader.

Subentries are critical components of science and medical indexing. These additional levels assist readers in refining their information search. In the previous examples, the main entries lack specificity and serve only as general markers for material. Samples from the full entries show the utility of subentries:

Abdomen, 15*f*
    arteries of, 722, 726*f*
    definition of, 14
    innervation of, 420
    regions of, 14–15, 16*f*
    transverse section through, 17*f*
    veins of, 734, 735*f,* 736*f,* 736*t,* 737*f*

volcanoes, 157–191
    activity, nature of, 159–170
    benefits of, 158–159
    caldera of, 167–170, 170*f*
    cinder cone, 165
    and climate, 115–116, 181
    composite cone, 167, 167*f*
    craters of, 167, 167*f*
    definition of, 165, 166*f*
    hot spot, 160, 161*f,* 163–164, 168–169
    plate tectonics and, 114–115, 114*t,* 160–162, 161*f*
    shield, 165–167, 166*f,* 167*f*
    subduction zone, 160, 161*f,* 163
    types of, 165–167

Electron(s), 34-36
    in Bohr model, 250–254, 250*f*
    charge of, 35–36, 35*f,* 36*f,* 38–39, 39*t*
    diffraction of, 254, 255*f,* 256–257
    discovery of, 34–36
    dot representation in Lewis structures, 325, 327–328
    emission, in photoelectric effect, 244–248, 244*f*
    gaining and losing, ions from, 40–41
    interference of, 254–257, 255*f*
    in quantum mechanical model, 237, 259–280
    sharing, in covalent bonds, 59, 60, 60*f*
    transfer of
        in ionic bonds, 59, 59*f,* 327
        in oxidation–reduction reactions, 116, 116*f*
    transitions of, 250–252, 250*f*

As mentioned earlier, subentries below the third level should be cause for concern. A reader has to wade through many entries before reaching a fourth level. Readers get lost and cannot do effective readbacks. I would not rule out fourth levels in all cases, but they should be used very sparingly.

Cross-references can be signposts at crucial junctions in the index. For the indexer, they can prevent excessive levels of subentries and save space. For the reader, they provide guidance to the information they originally sought or even indicate new topics to explore. I sometimes use broad cross-references from the most general entry if I believe the reader may require a nudge in the right direction. In a medical or anatomy text that includes a general entry like *Abdomen*, I might add a generic cross-reference like *See also specific procedures and disorders*. Samples of more specific cross-references I used in the earlier examples include:

> mudflows
>> volcanoes and. *See* volcanic mudflows
> volcanoes
>> eruptions of. *See* volcanic eruptions
>> St. Helens, Mount (Washington). *See* St. Helens, Mount, volcano
> Washington
>> St. Helens, Mount, volcano. *See* St. Helens, Mount, volcano

> Electron(s)
>> configuration in orbitals. *See* Electron configurations
>> orbitals of. *See* Orbital(s), atomic
> Geometry
>> electron. *See* Electron geometry

The structure of an index remains dynamic throughout the indexing process. Main entries can be altered or added; subentries can be expanded and deleted, and cross-references can be reworded and verified again. When the outlining or over-indexing tendency takes over, the indexer should walk away from the keyboard, reassess, and refresh, and then return to the task with the needs of the reader at the forefront of her mind.

WHY

With the subject matter mastered (or at least wrestled into submission) and the draft index completed, the indexer must contend with the question of *why*. In the editing process, the indexer has the opportunity to judge all the decisions made earlier. The indexer should read the index from beginning to end, assessing for coherence and consistency. The issue of professional judgment becomes paramount. An experienced indexer once told me that our choices are valid if we can explain why we made them. Of course, our reasoning must be sound, and above all other justifications our purpose is guiding and assisting the reader. The ideal editing process would include an honest and meaningful peer review. Unfortunately, the time constraints of our industry make this impractical for each and every index. If you are lucky to have talented peers around you as I do, quick consults on tricky issues are helpful, and periodic reviews (perhaps during those lulls we all fear) may be feasible. Despite our best intentions, we all develop troublesome habits over time. Complacency is not compatible with excellent indexing.

Space constraints demanded by the changing economic realities of publishing also force the indexer to make difficult choices. Sometimes the answer to why this is here and why something else is omitted is answered because space would not permit both. The indexer sometimes must deviate from the ideal for subentries and page references in order to consolidate entries and save lines. When facing these unhappy circumstances, the indexer should work with the author to retain the most user-friendly index possible.

HOW

With the intention of developing skills and advancing in the profession, the indexer finally must answer the question of *how*. The medical and science indexer should build on each and every experience. I shudder to think about the quality of the entries I generated that very first day of my tryout. Years from now I probably will detest the index I completed yesterday. But perhaps that is what I should hope for: continuing education and lifelong improvement. So how do we become better medical and science indexers?

Each new project presents unique challenges and opportunity for growth. My subspecialty in botany developed unexpectedly. A highly respected botanical research center was seeking someone to index a text on the genetics of plants. I had never tried botany before, but human genetics had been a common topic in my medical indexes. So I dared to take on the genetics of plants, and several botany texts have come my way since as a result. Indexers should expand their knowledge base whenever possible—through our work but also by reading voraciously. I cannot say I read medical journals or scientific papers after long days of indexing. But I seek scientific information in the mainstream media and occasionally research topics of interest more deeply.

My own indexes and models from other indexers also provide a basis for reflection and improvement. Once time has passed, even our own indexes appear differently to us. While the flaws seem to stand out, we sometimes spy something we appreciate. Reading someone else's index gives us a glimpse into a different thought process and sometimes inspires us to try a new approach. From a practical standpoint, a medical and science indexer should keep careful records and retain an archive of previous jobs. New editions sometimes only add a little new information or shift material. The old index may require only slight tweaking.

Finally, each indexer needs to fight to stay relevant in the changing publishing marketplace. Expanding your skill set or challenging yourself to apply your existing talents in a new way makes you more valuable and gives you greater resilience.

CONCLUSION

I came to indexing by necessity, but I discovered a profession that aspires to inform and educate. I fell into medical and science indexing through chance, but I found a specialty that satisfies my intellectual curiosity and challenges my organizational skills. My journalism background has proven central to my indexing career. I marvel at the dovetailing of my two vocations. Indexers convey information with the judicious and careful usage of words. Through the application of the 5Ws + H of journalism, I believe most indexers can overcome their hesitancy and enter the field of hard-science indexing with the determination and confidence to succeed.

Chapter 9

Indexing Math: Anyone Can Index Math, Right? After All, It's Only Numbers

Cynthia Landeen © 2014

The term *mathematics* covers an enormous range including basic math, geometry, pre-algebra, algebra, trigonometry, statistics, differential equations, and calculus. In addition, we have specialty math categories such as business math and technical math, and math for different professions including math for accountants, computer scientists, economists, engineers, nurses, pharmacy techs, real-estate agents, and even physicists. All of these have one thing in common: They all use the formal, man-made, specialized language of math.

I, myself, am a generalist indexer who when asked what types of books I index reply by saying it's more what I don't index. My standard response is "I don't index cookbooks, legal, Western medicine, or straight philosophy, although I do index quite a bit of Catholic theological philosophy." I believe that indexers are smart and dedicated to their craft. Given elbow grease, Wikipedia, and a deadline, most indexers can handle subjects about which they know very little. I once successfully took on a book on medieval mystery plays thinking I was getting a fun little book on fictional mysteries set in the Middle Ages. But I have repaired enough math indexes for despairing editors to believe that indexing math is different.

Indexing using the language of math, regardless at what level, is like indexing in a foreign language. If you're considering indexing math, and you're not a "maths person" as the Brits say, the first thing you should consider is if you know enough of the language to be certain the index you create will be accurate. If you're not certain of this, you probably don't. In that case, you need to either learn the language, if you have the time, or recommend the editor find another indexer. And, since most editors are also not "maths" people, they only discover they have a bad index once they have been roundly trounced by the author, and now everyone is either mad or in trouble.

For those of you from other backgrounds, it might be helpful to view this from another perspective. The following excerpt from Irving Conde Tullar's excellent article on indexing medicine illustrates how the specific can make a difference:

> [T]o list a series of parallels: *Champagne, champagne, sparkling wine,* and *method champenoise* all differ; as do *South* America, *Hispanic* America, and *Latin* America. *Bus desegregation* is not the same as *busing for desegregation.* The language we usually refer to as *Spanish* is more precisely *Castilian,* especially when referring to it in either Catalonia (*Catalan*) or Galacia (*Galician*); *Russia* and the *Soviet Union* differ historically, geographically, and politically. All *English* are *British,* but not all *British* are *English,* as most Arabs may be Muslim but most Muslims are not Arab; *Canadians* and *Mexicans* are also *North* Americans. The *Ottoman Empire,* the *Sublime Porte,* and *Turkey* are all related but not interchangeable terms. You should distinguish between *Christians, Orthodox Christians, Coptic Christians, Roman Catholics, Protestants, Baptists, Anabaptists,* and *Evangelists.* And sometimes it might even be, as Voltaire said of the Holy Roman Empire, that it "was neither holy, Roman, nor an empire." [From "General Medicine" (Irving Conde Tullar) from *Indexing Specialties: Medicine,* edited by L. Pilar Wyman]

With these cautions in mind, the focus of this article is on elementary-school level mathematics which includes basic geometry. It's a good place to start as most of us know the basics of the language. It's the specifics that can catch you out. Using definitions and examples, I plan to help you avoid what I have found to be the most common errors I've come across when repairing math indexes, and to give you a basic understanding of the language.

ANGLES

Let's start learning how this all works by first setting out definitions and then analyzing an entry for angles:

- Angle: A figure formed by two rays that have a common endpoint.

- Line: An infinitely extending one-dimensional figure that has length but not breadth or thickness.

- Ray: A portion of a line that originates at a point and goes on forever in only one direction.

- Vertex of an angle: The common endpoint of the two rays that form an angle.

Following is an example of a typical entry for angles. It contains subentries both for types of angles and information about angles. To create a correct entry you need to understand the definition of an angle and know about types of angles so they can be double posted as main entries:

angles *[typical entry by non-math indexer]*
    acute
    adjacent
    central
    classifying
    complementary
    congruent
    consecutive
    corresponding
    dihedral
    exterior
    interior
    interior of
    measuring
    naming
    nonadjacent
    obtuse
    perpendicular bisector
    reflex
    right
    sides of
    straight
    supplementary
    vertex
    vertical

Following is a better way to index angles (two entries—one with information about angles, and one for types of angles):

angles *[an entry for information about angles]*
    classifying
    exterior of
    interior of

> measuring
> naming
> perpendicular bisector
> of polygons
> sides of
> of triangles
> vertex of
>
> angles, types of *[all of these subentries are double posted as main entries]*
> acute
> adjacent
> central
> complementary
> congruent
> consecutive
> corresponding
> dihedral
> exterior
> interior
> nonadjacent
> obtuse
> reflex
> right
> straight
> supplementary
> vertical

BASE

Following are entries you might consider beginning with *base*. Before deciding how to sort these correctly, you'll need to understand some definitions:

- Exponent: The power to which a number, symbol, or expression is to be raised.

- Geometry: The branch of mathematics dealing with spatial relationships.

- Polygon: A plane figure bounded by straight edges.

- Prism: A three-dimensional figure with two parallel, congruent bases.

- Pyramid: A three-dimensional figure with a polygon for its base and triangles for its lateral faces.

- Three-dimensional: Having depth as well as height and width.

- Triangle: A three-sided polygon.

For a simple text this might be all the entry you need:

base
    three-dimensional objects
    two-dimensional objects

For a more complex text, entries can be grouped, and then followed by the numerical bases (from the definition, you know that geometric refers to relationships, so both two-dimensional and three-dimensional objects can be collected here):

base (geometric)
    angles of an isosceles triangle
    angles of a trapezoid
    of cone
    of cylinder
    of parallelogram
    of prism
    of pyramid
    of triangle
base five
base ten
base three
base twelve
base two

In an extremely complex text with extensive subentries, glosses will quickly and easily identify for the reader which use of base you're referring to:

base (of angle)
base (exponential)
base (two-dimensional objects)
base (numeration systems)
base (three-dimensional objects)

CENTER AND CENTROID

Following are a few entries you might find beginning with *center*. As always, understanding the definitions creates the parameters on how to sort the entries:

- Circle: A set of points in a plane equidistant from a single point, the circle's center.

- Centroid: The point where the three medians of a triangle meet.

- Isometry: A transformation that doesn't change the size or shape of the original object.

- Rotation: An isometry that spins an object about a fixed point.

- Sphere: A three-dimensional shape in which every point on its surface is equidistant from a single point, the sphere's center.

Here is a correct example, from a very basic text:

center
    of circle
    of sphere

Here is an incorrect example:

center
    of circle
    of sphere
    of rotation

The subentry *of rotation* would be incorrect as it refers to a function, not a shape. Instead you would want it as a main entry. The correct example would be:

center
    of circle
    of sphere
centers of rotation
centroid of triangle

It might be tempting to think of a centroid as a center if you were unfamiliar with the definitions, but it is a straightforward difference involving lines, not sets of points.

COMMON

While *common* is an adjective in most types of indexing, in math indexing the combination of terms beginning with *common* are nouns. All entries beginning with *common* are independent.

An incorrect entry would be:

common
    denominator
    difference
    factor
    multiple
    ratio

The correct entry is:

common denominator
common difference
common factor
common multiple
common ratio

DEGREE

Even though these entries refer to different uses of the term *degree*, the subentry format is correct in both examples:

degree
    angle
    minute
    second
    of temperature

degrees Celsius
degrees Fahrenheit

EQUAL AND EQUIVALENT

When indexing, always keep in mind that *equal* and *equivalent* are not the same. Following is an example:

equal-additions
equal differences
equality
equally likely
equal products
equal quotients
equal sets
equals sign
equal to
equivalence
equivalent
equivalent fractions
equivalent sets

HEIGHT AND ALTITUDE

To be mathematically correct, *height* refers to three dimensional objects, while *altitude* refers to polygons. Altitude is used almost exclusively with triangles.

LINES

There are all kinds of line entries. One way to check these entries is simply to try the entry using *lines* vs. *line*. *Lines graphs* doesn't make sense, thus making it a main entry. The only quirky thing about lines are number lines which, while lines, refer to the numbers found along a line. Therefore, a *See also* reference from *lines* to *See also number lines* would be appropriate. Here is an example:

line(s)
    angle bisector
    concurrent
    intersection
    number
    parallel
    perpendicular
    in a plane
    point-slope equation
    regression
    skewed
    slope-intercept equation
    slope of
    transversal

line graphs
line of reflection
line of symmetry
line plots
line segments

NUMBERS, NUMERALS, AND NUMERATION SYSTEMS

It might seem that in a math index you might not need entries beginning with *number*, but there are types of numbers and things about numbers that are important. First, there are types of numbers:

- Counting number: A positive integer.

- Integer: An element of the infinite and numerable set; this includes zero and negative numbers. Most of us think of this as whole numbers.

- Natural number: A positive integer.

- Prime number: A natural number greater than one, divisible only by itself and one.

- Rational number: A real number that can be expressed as the ratio of two integers.

- Real numbers: Includes the rational numbers and the irrational numbers, but not all complex numbers.

- Whole numbers: See *integer*.

Number(s)

The main entry number(s) requires a lot of either *See also* references or *See* references from the subentries depending on the complexity of the text:

number(s)
    abundant
    binary
    compatible
    composite
    counting. *See* integers
    decimal. *See* decimals
    deficient
    even

    figurate
    fractions. *See* fractions
    integers. *See* integers
    irrational
    law of large (LLN)
    lucky
    mixed
    multiple
    natural. *See* integers
    negative
    neighbor
    oblong
    odd
    palindromic
    pentagonal
    perfect
    positive
    prime. *See* prime numbers
    rational. *See* rational numbers
    real. *See* real numbers
    regrouping
    rounding
    whole. *See* integers
  number lines
  number mysticism
  number patterns
  number theory

Numeral

A numeral is a symbol that is not a word and represents a number. Although it's common to think of numbers and numerals in the same way, you can see from the definition that they are different and require their own entry. Examples of numerals are Roman numerals, and an entry might look like this:

    numerals
    Braille
    fractions as
    Roman
    word names for

Numeration Systems

A numeration system is any system of giving names to numbers:

> numeration systems
>> Babylonian
>> base-five
>> base-ten
>> Egyptian
>> Roman

POLYGONS AND REGULAR POLYGONS

As always, I begin with the definitions:

- Polygon: A plane figure bounded by straight edges.

- Regular Polygon: A polygon that's both equilateral and equiangular.

The trick to polygons is understanding, first, what a polygon is and, second, where to place them in the index. From the definition, you can see that polygons are two-dimensional figures and that they are bounded which indicates a closed shape. So, figures with three sides or more, even if irregular in shape, are polygons. Polygonal figures receive their own main entry without the use of *See also* references. For an example, on indexing specific types of polygons, take a look at the *triangle* entry. To make it slightly more complicated, regular polygons have equal sides and equal angles. Here's a typical entry for polygons:

> polygons
>> angles of
>> arbitrary
>> congruent
>> convex
>> diagonal
>> perimeter of
>> similar
>> tessellations
>> vertices

What you'll notice is that no polygonal form is included in this entry. Polygonal figures are given their own main entries.

Regular polygons are usually found as both a subentry to polygons and as their own main entry:

regular polygons
> angle measures *[perhaps each of the angle measures will have their own subentry]*
> Euclidean construction
> tessellations with

PROPERTIES

Properties might seem like they should be capitalized, but they aren't. While you don't need to know the definition of the properties, you do want to index them correctly. Quite often the properties are indexed as *property for*, but should be indexed as *property of*. If a property refers to more than one mathematical function, it can be indexed as two main entries or as one main entry with two subentries depending on the complexity of the text and whether sub-subentries are acceptable for index style:

associative property
> of addition
> division and
> with fractions
> of multiplication
closure property
> of addition
> division and
> of multiplication
> of subtraction
commutative property
> of addition
> division and
> with fractions
> of multiplication
> subtraction and
distributive property
identity property
> of addition
> of multiplication
similarity property *[isn't a true property and should be entered as similarity properties]*
zero property

Like *similarity property*, the entry *zero property* isn't a true property and should be entered as either:

    Zero
        division property of
        as identity property

or, depending on the text:

    zero-product property

Properties are also double posted under the mathematical function. Here's an example using sub-subentries:

    multiplication, properties of
        associative
        cancellation
        closure
        commutative
        distributive
            over addition
            over subtraction
        identity

THREE-DIMENSIONAL FIGURES OR SHAPES

Three-dimensional figures are handled in the same way as polygons, without *See also* references. While there is general information in the main entry, individual figures have their own main entry:

    three-dimensional shapes
        curved
        skew lines
        surface area
        volume

Examples of three-dimensional shapes are:

    cones
        surface area
        volume

cubes
    in base 10 manipulatives
    surface area
    volume
pyramids
    surface area
    volume

TWO-DIMENSIONAL FIGURES

By now, I hope it is evident that two-dimensional figures are either open or closed. Open two-dimensional figures are angles, and closed two-dimensional figures are polygons.

TRIANGLES

A triangle is a polygon with three sides and three angles. What you'll notice is different in the *triangle* entry is that types of triangles are included, unlike the polygon entries. Types of triangles are listed as subheads of the main entry and are *not* given their own main entry. This requires that you know what the types of triangles are. A typical entry is:

triangle(s)
    acute
    altitude
    arbitrary
    area
    base
    centroid *[wouldn't want to miss this subentry, as you learned earlier]*
    circumcenter
    congruent
    equilateral
    harmonic
    inequality
    isosceles
    legs
    Pascal's
    right
    scalene
    sum of angles

So there you have it—the basics. From here, you can only get better.

Chapter 10

The Heart of the Matter: An Introduction to the Challenges of Periodical Indexing

Linda S. Dunn © 2014

A periodical is "any publication that appears under the same title in consecutive parts (each part distinguished by a date or number) and that is expected to continue" (Booth 2001, 188).

There are many different types of periodicals with many different names: journals (literary, scholarly, scientific, academic, professional, or trade), magazines, newspapers, newsletters, annual reports, minutes (recordings of what took place in meetings of all kinds), and yearbooks are the most familiar kinds (Booth 2001, 186). Despite the differences in their names, content, publication frequency, and so on, all types share certain characteristics: Each periodical is a collection of documents, published in multiple issues, and provides special challenges to indexers (Booth 2001, 199–205). The challenges are intrinsically related to the special qualities of periodicals. Because each periodical title and issue contains a variety of different types of documents the indexer must choose which of them to index. Multiple issues require detailed locators in order to access a particular document. The many different writers will mean multiple variations in vocabulary, making the creation of a controlled vocabulary essential. And the ongoing nature of a periodical's publication limits the number of subject entries assigned to each document. Rather than exhaustivity, subject entries should provide pointers to the overall information or "aboutness" of documents.

In this chapter, the reader will quickly find that some of the periodical indexing principles and methods discussed are different from those of book indexing (Weaver 2002, 16). To begin, I will present the theoretical basis for these differences illuminated by Susan Klement in her 2002 article in *The Indexer* and then describe the four most important challenges of periodical indexing: what to index, locators, controlled vocabulary, and aboutness. The remainder of the chapter will

117

discuss practical rules and guidelines for determining aboutness, assigning subjects, and using subheadings. These challenges with their solutions are at the heart of the matter of periodical indexing.

Periodical indexes come in several formats, most of which use some sort of indexing software (Weaver 2002, 16):

- Print: Either included in an issue of a periodical title or in a separate publication.

- Online: On a periodical title's website or some other related site.

- Databases: Compilers or aggregators of periodical indexes. They will likely include many different periodical indexes, each of which indexes hundreds of periodical titles. In general, the indexing principles for each format are the same. If there is a difference in a particular area of periodical indexing, I will mention it in that context.

It is difficult to recognize a concept that has not been distinctly named (Klement 2002, 23).

THEORY OF PERIODICAL INDEXING
Periodical Indexes Are Open Systems

Klement's article "Open-System Versus Closed-System Indexing: A Vital Distinction" appeared in the April 2002 issue of *The Indexer*. In the article, she developed a conceptual framework, as well as a carefully defined vocabulary, in order to describe the different requirements for book and periodical indexes. Her very detailed explanation of the differences between the systems is laid out in a table comparing 42 characteristics of each system. She argues that distinguishing periodical indexes from book indexes is important because different indexing processes are required. She labels the two systems as "closed" or "open" systems (Klement 2002, 23). A back-of-the-book index is a closed system because it is complete in itself, will not be added to in the future, and when it is finished will remain closed. Periodical indexes are open systems because:

- They are never finished.
- They go on indefinitely.
- They are constantly evolving.

Open systems must, therefore, have different indexing rules and procedures (Weaver 2002, 16). Among the 42 characteristics, three create the most challenges and will be the focus of this chapter:

- Locators must include the periodical title and issue information as well as page numbers.

- Subject terms should be organized into a controlled vocabulary/thesaurus, which is kept up to date.

- Periodical indexing involves determining the aboutness of each indexable unit.

I will begin with one more challenge not directly addressed in Klement. When creating a periodical index, the first decision is which documents to index in each periodical title (Russell 2008, 4).

WHAT TO INDEX

The term *article* has a specific definition in periodical language referring to longer essays about a topic. Therefore, I am going to use the term *indexable unit* as the general name for every document or unit of content in a periodical issue (Anderson 1997, 11–12).

There are many types of indexable units in addition to articles (Booth 2001, 189–199). The possibilities depend to some extent on the focus of each periodical title:

- Art journals: Reviews of art exhibitions, interviews, and articles on artists

- Celebrity magazines: Interviews, photographs, and news items

- Literary journals: Cover art, poems, film or play scripts, short stories, and reviews of books, films, and plays

- Political or news periodicals: Cartoons, editorials, letters to the editor, and historical essays

- Newspapers: Editorials, calendars, and advertisements

- Trade journals about equipment: Product news and surveys

All of the articles in each periodical title should, of course, be indexed, but what about all that other material? Which of it is worth indexing? This will depend on the type of periodical and the intentions of the index publisher. What may be important to index in one kind of periodical may not be appropriate in another (Booth 2001,

200; Weaver 2002, 19). This is a decision which should be made by the indexer in consultation with the publisher.

After these decisions have been made, the indexer should continue to watch out for changes in the unit lengths, check for the addition of new indexable units, and keep an eye out for changes in format, periodical titles, numbering systems, and so on. For example, I once indexed a journal in which the very short film reviews of a paragraph or so were not indexed. But, eventually, the film reviews grew to column length and the decision to include them in the index was made.

CREATING LOCATORS AND CITATIONS

Locators for periodical indexes must include the periodical title, a numbering system which identifies the particular periodical issue, and the pagination. The locator plus an indexable unit's author(s) and title is called the *citation* (Booth 2001, 201).

Expert Tip

If the periodical index (like most databases) contains more than one periodical title, the titles of the indexed periodicals must be included in the citation. If the periodical index is limited to only one periodical title, the title of the periodical is not required.

A standard format for citations is not well established for periodical indexing (Weaver 2002, 20), but the authority that I use is *Bibliographic references Z39.29-2005* (hereafter referred to as ANSI/NISO *Bibliographic references*) published by the American National Standards Institute (ANSI)/National Information Standards Organization (NISO) (see the references for how to obtain a copy of this document). This standard includes solutions to the many variables of periodical citations. Here is the recommended order of the citation with the suggested punctuation:

Authorship. Title of indexable unit. Periodical title. date; volume (issue): pagination

Expert Tip

Entire books have been devoted to the creation of controlled vocabularies and thesauri. For example, the ANSI/NISO *Guidelines for the Construction, Format, and Management of Monolingual Controlled Vocabularies*, 2005, is 184 pages long.

The standard allows for one change in the order of the citation: "Any bibliographic element, such as a title or a date of publication, may be moved to another place in a reference, as long as that element appears in the same place in all references in the list and as long as the order of the remaining elements appears as specified by the standard" (ANSI/NISO *Bibliographic references* 2005, 58). I choose to move the date and put the journal title (if needed) in italics with no period after it. For example:

Smith, Robert. Researching your research paper on the Internet. *College Research Libraries* 59(3):212–218 May 1988

This arrangement of the citation more closely matches the practices of databases and well-respected periodical indexes. It makes the most sense to me because the volume and issue number are together and the date and year are at the end. This is the format we used at the *Film Literature Index* where I worked, and I will use it in the examples given in this chapter unless the source of the citations differs greatly. If the index is for a periodical title which has changed its name during the course of publication or for more than one periodical title, the indexer and publisher may decide to use abbreviations for the periodical titles. Sources for standard abbreviations for periodical titles can be found in the references section.

In these days of databases and linked full text, users often don't really notice the citation. When they find a citation they wish to consult, a click on the Full Text button automatically delivers that article. Nevertheless, the citation is still needed to identify the source of the unit and also to provide the "citation" for papers written using that unit as a source.

ORGANIZING SUBJECT TERMS INTO A CONTROLLED VOCABULARY OR THESAURUS

A *controlled vocabulary* is a collection of preferred subject terms that are chosen from the language of the periodical(s) being indexed and authorized to be used as the subject terms for the periodical index. *See* references from any synonyms to the authorized terms are an important component (ANSI/NISO *Controlled Vocabularies*, 5).

A *thesaurus* is a controlled vocabulary that is organized hierarchically and also has relational structures between the authorized terms (Anderson 1997, 19). This means there are broader and narrower terms as well as equivalent terms that are related to each other. *See also* references from broader to narrower terms and between related terms are used as well as *See* references (Anderson 1997, 43).

Source of Subject Terms

Although the vocabulary for periodical indexes initially comes from the indexable units, a thesaurus should be the source of the subject terms for the indexing process. As a result the thesaurus provides the structure of the index as well as the control of the subject terms. According to ANSI/NISO *Controlled Vocabularies*, a thesaurus is based on four principles of vocabulary control: "eliminating ambiguity, controlling synonyms, establishing relationships among terms where appropriate, and testing and validation of terms" (ANSI/NISO *Controlled Vocabularies*, 12). My discussion of thesaurus creation in this chapter will be based on those principles in a slightly different order interspersed with the rules for the formats for the various types of authorized vocabulary.

Validation of Terms

The validation or verification of subject terms is the first step in controlling the vocabulary of a periodical index. In the initial creation of the index, and as an ongoing procedure, any terms considered for inclusion in the thesaurus should be verified, if possible, in some reputable or standard CV, thesaurus, dictionary, or other reference work (ANSI/NISO *Controlled Vocabularies*, 16). If no verification is possible, but the term is used consistently in the periodical(s) being indexed, then the indexer may use this consistent usage as the basis for authorizing the term for use in the thesaurus. This is a very important part of the development of a periodical index. Without the authorization process for a thesaurus, inconsistency of terms about the same concept develops rather quickly. This can cause a lot of work for indexers who may have to guess which term to use—and also causes a messy index (Weaver 2002, 19–20). The authorization of terms will also help the creator of the thesaurus decide which if any synonymous terms should be chosen as the preferred term based on the context of the periodical title (see the next topic "Synonym Control"). The verification process may also suggest related and hierarchical terms as well (see later in the chapter, "Establishing Relationships Among Terms Where Appropriate").

If you have the resources, the use of a focus group or subject expert review may prove even more on point with your intended audience.

Synonym Control

Due to the variety and inconsistency of terms used in different periodicals as well as those in the indexable units within a periodical title, there may be more than one term used for the same concept. During the authorization process the indexer must choose one of the terms as the authorized one (Klement 2002, 24; Wellisch 1994, 623), and make any other terms with similar meanings into *See* references for the authorized term (Anderson 1997, 18; ANSI/NISO *Controlled Vocabularies*, 44–45). Here are some examples of *See* references from synonyms to authorized terms:

> 19th century. *See* nineteenth century
> cars. *See* automobiles
> lifts. *See* elevators
> madness. *See* insanity

Using Formal vs. Everyday Language

In general, controlled vocabulary subject terms for periodicals should be in common usage. The authorized terms should be familiar to the people reading the specific periodical title or used in the subject area of the title. They should not be too formal or old fashioned, but also not terms that the creator judges are slang or terms that won't last.

According to ANSI/NISO *Controlled Vocabularies* slang or jargon terms may be used in a controlled vocabulary if the terms "cover new concepts originating within a particular specialty, subculture, or social group. When no widely accepted alternative exists, the neologism, slang, or jargon term should be accepted as a term" (ANSI/NISO *Controlled Vocabularies*, 31–32). These slang terms come from the *Film Literature Index*:

> blockbusters
> demo reels
> pitching
> runaway production

Singular or Plural Subject Terms

Which subject terms should be singular or plural is a decision that must be made in the beginning and then followed consistently. The rule in *Guidelines for Indexes* is as follows: "It is the convention and custom to use the plural form for terms denoting discrete objects (countables) and the singular form for mass terms and most abstract expressions (noncountables)" (Anderson 1997, 15). When you can ask the question "how many" about a subject term then the plural is used. The singular is used when you can ask the question "how much?"

Examples of countables:	Examples of noncountables:
automobiles in film	film
directors	modernism
sets and set designs	philosophy

Foreign Words

Subject terms that have become acceptable usage in English (known as "loan words") can become authorized terms in a thesaurus. If there are non-English terms used in the periodical that have not become naturalized, then those terms should become *See* references to the authorized terms (ANSI/NISO *Controlled Vocabularies*, 33–34):

Examples of acceptable loan words are:

Cineaste
Coup d'etat
Habeas corpus
Pas de deux

Eliminating Ambiguity

There are two primary ways to distinguish subject terms that have different meanings or need modification in order to be specific enough for the index. These additions to the authorized terms are known as qualifiers and modifiers.

Qualifiers for Subject Terms

Qualifiers are words, usually enclosed in parentheses, that differentiate between subject terms with multiple meanings (ANSI/NISO *Controlled Vocabularies*, 20–21). They are very helpful when needed but should not be used unless absolutely necessary. For example:

$$
\text{Mercury} \begin{cases} \text{car} \\ \text{metal} \\ \text{mythological character} \\ \text{planet} \end{cases}
$$

If the periodicals you are indexing are focused on a single topic such as cars or astronomy, then the parenthetical qualifier may not be necessary. But when you are indexing a periodical with a wide range of topics or a number of periodicals with different subjects, some qualifiers will be required. Here is another example of qualifiers. Note that some qualifiers are more conceptual in nature:

fans (accessories)
fans (cooling equipment)
fans (persons)

creation (literary, artistic, etc.)
family values (concept)

Modifiers for Subject Terms

Modifiers are usually adjectives or adjective-like parts of speech that, when combined with the subject term, make it more specific. *Controlled Vocabularies* has a lot to say about how to use modifiers when constructing compound terms as there are many possible situations requiring modifiers (ANSI/NISO *Controlled Vocabularies*, 36–42). Here, I will only discuss their use in creating more specific subject terms and a few examples of their formatting.

Examples of subject terms with modifiers are:

adult audiences
African-American women authors *[two modifiers!]*
public television
women screenwriters

In the past, modified terms were often inverted in periodical indexes (*audience, adult*). This is no longer so commonly done. Instead the inversions are made into *See* references. This is the same in both print indexes and databases. In terms with multiple modifiers, multiple *See* references should be made:

authors, African-American women. *See* African-American women authors
women authors, African-American. *See* African-American women authors

Another type of compound term, also made up of two or more words, are those terms that appear in everyday language. These terms should be entered into the thesaurus in their original format or their meaning will be lost. Inversions of these everyday language compound terms may be given *See* references from their inversions (ANSI/NISO *Controlled Vocabularies*, 41). Here are some compound terms which appear in everyday language:

Flying buttresses
Stained glass

Phrases as Subject Terms and the Use of Function Words

Sometimes a subject concept cannot be conveyed with only a single term plus qualifiers or modifiers. I call these *phrase terms*. Phrase terms are constructed from authorized terms joined together with function words (ANSI/NISO *Controlled Vocabularies*, 25). When creating these types of terms, which might be applicable to other topics as well, it is very important to be consistent in their terminology. In these examples, the creator of the index chose to create two types of phrase terms, which can then be used for any topic in film or in literature:

> Africa in film *[references to films in film]*
> Africa in literature *[references to films in literature]*

The phrase terms that follow come from common English usage. It is a good idea to check subject terms like these in a reliable source to be certain that they are created in the way they should be written or spelled as they can be misspelled by the authors of the various indexable units:

> Plaster of Paris
> Sergeants-of-Arms

Unlike book indexes, terms in thesauri for periodical indexes should never end in prepositions. Just as a sentence should not end with a preposition, a periodical index subject term should not either. Therefore phrase terms should never be created as inversions; see the first column:

Avoid constructions like these:	Acceptable use in compound terms:
directors, actors as	actors as directors
literature, sailors in	sailors in literature

Modifiers, Qualifiers, and Phrase Terms in a Database

Compound terms should not be separated into their components for a database even though searching can be done by putting two or more words together (Anderson 1997, 15). The reason for this is that compound and phrase terms create a single concept that may not be returned by entering the components of the terms separately.

For example, separating the compound term *school libraries* and searching on the two words, you might also get *library schools*. Similarly, separating *birth control* could return a lot of articles that address these concepts in conjunction with each other but not the concept of *birth control* (Anderson 1997, 15).

Establishing Relationships Among Terms Where Appropriate

In addition to *See* references that are added for synonyms of the authorized subject terms, a thesaurus should also have hierarchical and associative relationships that are displayed in the index as *See also* references. Hierarchical relationships are those between broader (BT) and narrower (NT) terms. *Controlled Vocabularies* provide instructions for a number of different types of BT and NT relationships (ANSI/NISO *Controlled Vocabularies*, 46–51). It also explains the creation of associative or related subject terms (ANSI/NISO *Controlled Vocabularies*, 51–57).

First, here is an example of a thesaurus display:

Example of hierarchical relationships: **Example of associative relationships:**
Equines   Donkeys
   NT: Donkeys   BT: Equines
      Horses   RT: Horses
      Mules   Mules

And here is an example of an index display:

Example of hierarchical relationships:
Equines. *See also* Donkeys; Horses; Mules

Example of associative relationships:
Donkeys. *See also* Horses; Mules

The inclusion of these kinds of relationships among the subject terms helps both indexers and users find the most specific terms as well as terms they might not have realized were in the thesaurus.

To find out more about thesaurus creation, I highly recommend the two articles by Julia Marshall published in *Key Words* (the American Society for Indexing bulletin) and found in the references section. Also, the ANSI/NISO *Controlled Vocabularies* contains even more information than you thought you would ever need to create a CV or a thesaurus (see the references for how to obtain a copy of this document).

DETERMINING THE ABOUTNESS OF EACH INDEXABLE UNIT

An indexer must answer these two questions when considering each unit of indexable matter:

- What is the unit about as a whole?

- What are the most specific subjects that capture the particular aboutness of this unit?

Aboutness is the most important concept in the process of indexing periodicals—and the most challenging. I have used this term for years to explain the process of periodical indexing to new indexers. It pleased me to find that Klement uses the same term in her article (Klement 2001, 24). Aboutness means the subject(s) that encompasses the whole of an indexable unit (Booth 2001, 203). Deciding what the indexable unit is about requires stepping back from the individual parts of a unit and determining what subject(s) would apply to the entire unit. Is it about a person, a creative work, a place, and/or a subject term? More than one of each? Or some combination of these?

Aboutness of whole units is the most striking difference between periodical and book indexing (Klement 2002, 24). Unlike a book index that covers each significant reference to a person, place, or subject, the periodical index serves to point users in the right direction for information on their topics of interest (Klement 2002, 24). It does not and cannot indicate every occurrence of a name or a subject. Because the periodical index and the content being indexed have traditionally been separate, the indexer must make sure that the journey from citation to accessing the indexable unit merits the trip.

What steps go into determining the aboutness for an indexable unit? And how does the indexer then assign subjects to the unit? Here are some guidelines to help the indexer determine aboutness, followed by a discussion of how to assign subject entries.

Guidelines and Helpful Hints on Determining Aboutness

First, a cautionary note: Only very rarely should you need to read the entire unit (Klement 2002, 28). In fact, it is better not to, since doing so will invariably increase the temptation to over-index. I know this sentence will seem heretical to book indexers, but it is true nonetheless. In almost all cases, one or a combination of the places on the list that follows will give sufficient guidance to determine aboutness and its corresponding subject(s) for the indexable unit (Lancaster 1991, 19).

The guidelines discussed in this section will be more helpful as the indexer gains some experience in indexing a particular periodical title. In the beginning, she may need to read some of the units all the way through until she becomes familiar with the periodical's topics.

The parts of the indexable units discussed on the following pages will help to determine the whole unit's aboutness. Do not forget that the unit's aboutness could also be a person or a book or something equally straightforward. It is not necessary to go through all of these steps every time, just enough of them to provide a sense of what subject(s), personal or corporate names, and so on could be chosen. For some units, one look at the title will be enough (yes, I really do mean that). Some units will be more difficult or titles oblique, so you need to consult more unit parts. And you frequently encounter a few units for which going through the whole list still may not result in a grasp of the aboutness. Then you have to read part of the unit. (All of the examples in this section are from EBSCO's Film & Television Literature Index with Full Text.)

Start With the Title and Subtitle

Checking the unit title (if there is one) works well in scholarly and scientific journals where unit titles are chosen to give the reader a good sense of what the units cover (Booth 2001, 203). Some examples are:

> Baker, Victoria. Authors as collaborators: Scholarly works and indexer/author relations. *Key Words* 18(1):16–18 Jan–Mar 2010
> Motion picture film (35 mm): Camera aperture images and usage [proposed American National Standard]. *SMPTE Journal* 99:795–797 Sep 1990
> Sklar, Robert. To honor your country, criticize it: Amos Gitai's Israeli fiction films. *Cineaste* 35(4):19–23 Fall 2010

The first two titles are quite straightforward and clearly indicate what the units are about. The first is about collaboration between authors and indexers of their scholarly books. The second is about 35 mm motion picture film, 35 mm camera apertures, and American National Standards Institute standards. The third example has a subtitle that is helpful even though the first part of the title is not. Since these titles give what appears to be sufficient information, you can stop with this step and scan the unit quickly to make sure the title accurately reflects the aboutness of the unit.

You will, of course, face many unit titles that tell you nothing useful at all, including sometimes even the article titles in scholarly journals (Booth 2001, 204). Nevertheless, unit titles make a good place to start looking for aboutness. Here are examples of titles with no helpful information:

> Acumen, M. Finns carry thinner wallets. *Variety* 342:96 Feb 11 1991
>
> Green, E. All the world's a stage. *Sight & Sound* 20(11):14 Nov 2010

Taking either of these titles literally would get the indexer into difficulties. The first example actually deals with the Finnish film importers at a film festival—certainly not about wallets except as an allusion to money. The second example involves an actor in films, not theater productions.

Look at the Section Heading

The titles of columns or series that appear in nearly every issue of a periodical title (e.g., Editorial or Reviews) are known as *section headings* (also known as *departments* or *running head titles*). Often these titles are what appear in the table of contents. An example of a section heading is as follows:

Kalian, Paul. Video releases. *Cinema Papers* 52:36 Mar 1991

The section heading (which is also the title) for this unit tells us that the unit is about films released on video or DVD. Depending on the length of the unit, the aboutness could be the titles of the films, or you could assign a subject like *films on video*. Series or columns can be easy to index if they have the same aboutness in every issue. If they do not, those which are a miscellany of not much information on a number of subjects may fall into the category of omitted units.

Check Keywords

Keywords are uncontrolled words (not authorized by a person to be included in the thesaurus) often provided by the author and allowed as search terms by the users in a database (Anderson 1997, 39). Here is an example of keywords:

Wilson, Emma. Desire and technology: an interview with Atom Egoyan. *Film Quarterly* 64(1):29–37 Sep 2010
KEYWORDS: Atom Egoyan, *Chloe, Adoration*, digital, memory

Note that the keywords for this article include a person's name and two film titles. Do not, however, rely on the keywords without evaluation. Remember that keywords are not controlled vocabulary terms; they use natural language (Anderson 1997, 39). They may or may not be subjects that were chosen by the author, and they may not describe the aboutness of the whole indexable unit. Keywords may be useful, however, in pointing the indexer in the right direction or confirming preliminary aboutness ideas (Booth 2001, 207).

Check the Abstract

Let's look at an example from the same citation:

Wilson, Emma. Desire and technology: an interview with Atom Egoyan. *Film Quarterly* 64(1):29–37 Sep 2010
ABSTRACT: Armenian Canadian director Atom Egoyan's recent films, *Adoration* (2006) and *Chloe* (2009), and his art installations pursue and complicate his career-long interest in technology and its intersections with desire

and fantasy. In an interview with Emma Wilson, Egoyan discusses these works and reflects more broadly on filmmaking in the digital age.

This abstract is quite helpful; it agrees with the keywords that the unit deals with a director and two of his films. Approach abstracts, like keywords, cautiously. Even when written by the author, they may not be totally accurate. If someone else wrote the abstract, the person may have missed the point of the unit altogether. When they are good, though, they provide a very good place to look for clues about the unit (Weaver 2002, 18). Indexers should always check the abstract against their own thoughts about the unit's aboutness (Booth 2001, 205).

Check the Introduction and Conclusion

After a look at the unit title, subtitle, section headings, keywords, and/or abstract, confirm any acquired information on the unit's aboutness by checking the introduction and conclusion of the indexable unit. If the author has written a good introduction, he will have foreshadowed his central points. But also scan the concluding paragraphs to confirm that the author wrote about what he said he would (Booth 2001, 205).

A surprising number of people deviate from what they say they are going to write about, at least in the arts and humanities. And, unfortunately, some writers do not introduce their units well and/or fail to draw the unit to a conclusion at the end. They say they will address a topic in a certain way, but don't actually carry through with it and veer off to something else altogether. Or they wander all over the place without settling on anything. Sometimes these sorts of units are not even worth indexing. My favorite example of such a unit came in a French film magazine I used to index. Every month the author wrote in a poetic and disconnected way about all the films he had seen in the past month. It was not terribly interesting or informative, and we decided not to index it. As I recall, the title was something about the moon, which helps to explain a lot—very romantic and not down to earth; it was fun to read, but not to index. And it wouldn't have been of much help to a user either.

Scan the Unit

Remember the nonreading rule! With the ideas culled from the places just suggested, scan the unit very quickly to check whether the whole unit is really about those ideas. This advice generally applies to the really long articles of scholarly or research periodicals. A one-page unit should not need this kind of checking.

This is the moment to note that long scholarly articles are often easier to index than shorter units because they usually have good introductions and conclusions, addressing a specific topic at length, while short indexable units may cover a lot of topics very briefly.

ASSIGNING SUBJECT ENTRIES TO INDEXABLE UNITS

Subject entries for an indexable unit include the names of people, businesses or corporate bodies, and places; the titles of creative works; and/or subject terms.

Subject terms are the words or phrases naming concepts that have been collected into the thesaurus created for this periodical title(s). In many cases, people, businesses, and/or creative works such as books and films are the only subject entries for an indexable unit. Sometimes the unit may be about only subject terms. And sometimes the subject entries for a unit may include a combination of all the types of subject entries. A synonym for subject terms is *subject headings*.

Choosing the Most Specific Subject Entries

Remember the second question indexers should ask themselves: *What are the most specific subjects that capture the particular aboutness of this unit?*

What does *specificity* mean in regard to subject entries? While aboutness applies to the indexable unit as a whole, specificity applies to the choice of subject entries. A good, if short, definition of specificity by Gerard Salton that I found in Mulvany's book is that specificity is the "degree of breadth or narrowness of terms" (Mulvany 1994, 49). I have expanded this definition to include all types of subject entries for periodical indexing (Booth 2001, 203). Specificity means, therefore, that the indexer must choose the narrowest subject entries that will also apply to the unit as a whole (Anderson 1997, 12).

Specificity in subject terms is created by consistency in vocabulary and the relationships between terms in a thesaurus. There both the indexer and user can find broader and narrower term relationships that provide choices for the most specific terms available. If there is not a term specific enough, it should be added to the list of new terms to consider adding to the thesaurus. In this way the thesaurus continues to grow and reflect the documents more accurately.

Some Rules Governing the Choice of Subject Terms

The following three rules come from those used by the *Film Literature Index* and are based on the thesaurus structure. As discussed in the section on the organization of vocabulary, the thesaurus not only provides controlled vocabulary for a periodical index, it also creates the structure for the index through the relationships between the subject terms. To misuse the thesaurus, or to use it incorrectly, causes the integrity of the index to break down. Periodical indexes usually tend to the large side, so the root problem of the index is not easily recognizable. But in small indexes it shows up quite quickly in the *See also* references. If two related subject terms are both assigned to the same indexable unit, the *See also* references between those two terms will only lead to the same citation. With lots of citations this may never be noticed, but if there are not many, then the cross-references reveal the misuse of the thesaurus immediately.

An index's lack of structure makes it confusing for the users who may question their search methods. It is also confusing to the indexer. I have worked in situations like this and it is very frustrating. It is almost impossible to know how to assign the subject terms because the rules of assignment do not correspond to the thesaurus structure. I call this the dartboard method of periodical indexing. The indexer proceeds by choosing whatever subject terms he can find in the jumbled subject basket and throws them at the unit rather than starting with the article, determining its aboutness, and choosing the appropriate term. This is an example of the broader and narrower terms related to the rules and examples that follow:

War
American Civil War, 1861–1865

Narrower
Terms { Chancellorsville, Virginia (battle, 1863)
Gettysburg, Pennsylvania (battle, 1863)
Shiloh, Tennessee (battle, 1862)
Yorktown, Virginia (battle, 1862)

1. Two subject terms that are in a broader and narrower relationship in the thesaurus should not both be assigned to the same unit. An indexable unit is about the Battle of Gettysburg during the Civil War. Using the rule of specificity, the subject term *Gettysburg, Pennsylvania (battle, 1863)* should be chosen. This rule prohibits the assignment of the broader term as well, in this case, *American Civil War, 1861–1865*. It doesn't make sense to use both the broader and narrower term when the rule of specificity requires the use of the narrowest term applicable to the whole. Subject terms that are either related terms to *American Civil War, 1861–1865* or its broader term *war* should not be used with the more specific term either.

2. Two subject terms that are both narrower terms of the same broader term should not be assigned to the same unit. Using the same set of subject terms, another indexable unit discusses and compares two battles of the Civil War. The indexer may be tempted to use the most specific subject terms *Gettysburg, Pennsylvania (battle, 1863)* and *Yorktown, Virginia (battle, 1862)*. This rule prohibits that because of the rule of aboutness. A single unit cannot be about two related terms. In situations like this, I use what I call the "ladder of specificity."

What to do when the terms chosen for a unit turn out to be related by being narrower terms of the same broad term? It is very tempting to use the subjects terms for the two battles. As pointed out, the rule of the whole of an indexable unit takes precedence over the rule of specificity. The indexer should therefore retreat to the broader term *American Civil War.* I find the image of a ladder of subject terms very useful. Moving up and down the rungs of broader and narrower terms helps me to arrive at the most appropriate term. Many people do not like this rule and I understand why they don't. But, as I pointed out in the introduction to this section, it is integral to the organization of the index to respect the structure of the thesaurus. And it is only on rare occasions that this dilemma arises. Every unit of indexable content should have at least one subject entry assigned to it. If there doesn't seem to be even one entry to describe the aboutness of the unit, do not index it. I would also suggest that any rules created for indexing a periodical should not require any more entries than one. Requiring a larger number of entries can lead to superfluous subject entries in an effort to fulfill this requirement. Most units, no matter what types they are, will need only two or three entries including subject terms, names of a film, play, or book, and so on.

3. The rule of four or more governs the instances in which the indexer is tempted to assign four or more subject entries that are related to each other. For example, an article on documentary filmmakers may discuss a number of specific documentary filmmakers. If the article covers each director at length, then the indexer might consider those directors as the subject entries. The rule of four or more requires that, if there are four or more narrower entries, then the indexer should move up a rung of the specificity ladder to the broader level, which would be *documentary filmmakers.* (For instances like this, when parts of an article would be long enough to include the director's names, for example, see "Units Requiring Multiple Aboutnesses" later in this chapter.) Here is an example of the rule of four:

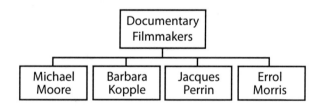

And further, the length of the unit does not mean more subject entries are necessary. In a two-page article on Martin Scorsese and the films that should have won him the Oscar, the author also mentions the actors who have appeared in many of Scorsese's films: It is "about" the director Martin Scorsese.

An article of 40 pages in a scholarly film journal in which the author discusses all the films Martin Scorsese has made in his career is "about" the director Martin Scorsese.

A two-page article in a technical journal on a new version of the color process Technicolor is "about" Technicolor film.

An article of 20 pages in a historical journal about the development and subsequent use of the color process in films of the 50s and 60s is "about" Technicolor film.

Units Requiring Multiple Aboutnesses

Now that I have emphasized the error of assigning too many subject entries, I will discuss an alternative solution to this rule. Sometimes, in long articles, the author devotes a number of pages to multiple subtopics. These subtopics often have a subtitle or are distinguished in some way from the body of the text. In the 40-page article about Martin Scorsese just mentioned, all of his films are discussed separately at some length within the article, each under the film's title. In cases like this, the indexer can use an alternative to the aboutness rule by creating additional and separate indexable units with the subtitles as the title of the new units. This satisfies the rule that limits the overall aboutness to the unit as a whole by dividing the article into smaller units in addition to the large article, which is also indexed.

Assigning Names and Places

Authority files are lists of any type of subject entries to be used in an index in which there are authorized entries and also *See* references from synonyms to the authorized entries (Anderson 1997, 36; Booth 2001, 207). Authority files can be created for personal names, corporate entries, or titles of creative works as well as any other subject entries required by the index. CVs or thesauri are the authority files for subject terms.

When deciding the aboutness for a particular unit, remember that names and places are also considered subject entries. An indexable unit can be entirely about a person or two, about people and corporations, about a place, about names and places, or about any of those in addition to subject terms. Depending on the type of periodical you are indexing, there may well be many more entries for names, places, and other nonsubject entries than for subject terms. Like subject terms, names of persons, corporations, governmental organizations, and places should also have their own authority files. Name and place authority files are not as elaborate as the thesaurus for subject terms. Names and places can even be integrated into the thesaurus, but I prefer to keep them separate from each other, especially when they become very large files. Like subject terms, qualifiers can be added to names and places to distinguish those that have identical names from each other

(Anderson 1997, 18; ANSI/NISO *Controlled Vocabularies*, 106). Here are some examples (Anderson 1997, 17):

> Metropolitan Museum of Art (Cleveland, OH)
> Metropolitan Museum of Art (New York, NY)

> Albany (NY)
> Albany (OR)

Assigning Titles of Creative Works

The same instructions apply to the titles of creative works such as books, plays, films, musical works, and so on as apply to names and places. The creative work title may be the only entry or it may accompany a person's name, subject term, or other type of entry. And the titles should follow standardized rules for their entry (Anderson, 1997, 18):

> *Charlemagne* (play)
> *Genesis* (Anglo-Saxon poem)

> *Ave Maria* (Schubert)
> *Ave Maria* (Verdi)

ADDING SUBHEADINGS TO THE INDEX

Subheadings are authorized or standardized subject terms that are used to create subdivisions in the main subject entries in an index. Subheadings are defined by Anderson and NISO as "a modifying heading subordinated to a main heading in a multi-level heading" (Anderson 1997, 42).

Multi-level headings are "a heading consisting of a main heading that is modified by a subheading. The subheading may in turn be modified by a sub-subheading and possibly by additional headings at successive levels of subordination" (Anderson 1997, 40).

All types of subheadings create greater specificity for their corresponding subject entries by providing more information on the subject entry. This is not only important for the rule of specificity but also makes the index much easier to use. A search that results in entries with a large number of citations assigned to it is not very helpful to users. They then have to scan the titles to see, for example, which indexable units are about a specific country or are a particular type of article. Or if the user wants a biography of Stephen King, she will not want lots of citations that are reviews of his books or comparisons of his work with other writers.

Methods of Applying Subheadings

There are several methods of adding subheadings. One way is to add them to the subject terms in the thesaurus. A database on which I have worked creates multi-level terms in this way. The problem with this system is that the *See* and *See also* references can be lost if the references are only applied to the main authorized subject terms without any subheadings. Then, if the indexer uses subject terms with subheadings, the references are not activated. And every time there is the need for a new subheading, a new term needs to be added to the thesaurus. Here are examples of multi-level subject headings from the Library of Congress (LOC) Authorities:

> Bibliography – Best books – Children's literature
> Birth control – United States – Periodicals
> Periodicals – Canada – Bibliography

Another way to apply subheadings is to add them to the subject entries during the indexing process. This method gives the indexer much more flexibility than attaching the subheadings to the subject terms. Subheadings can then be used with names and titles as well as any subject term to which they might apply. And since the *See* and *See also* references are attached to the subject terms with or without subheadings, they will not be lost when subheadings are used.

Following is a brief survey of the ways to create multilevel terms with subheadings. I will discuss three types of subheadings that can be used: general, geographic, and authorized subject subheadings. These subheadings can be used alone to modify an authorized subject entry or one type can be combined with another.

Helpful as subheadings are, show restraint in their usage. You do not need a subheading for every subject entry. Use them only when they increase the specificity of the subject term but without splitting the main subject term into too many splinters.

General Subheadings

General subheadings are created from subject-type terms or headings that are not used as authorized terms in the thesaurus. General subheadings are terms that can only be used as subheadings (and not as subject terms) in order to create more specific subject terms. They are called general subheadings because they can be used with any subject entry, including names, corporate names, and titles of creative works as well as with subject terms. General subheadings can also identify the type of indexable units. Examples of possible general subheadings are:

adults
children
interviews
maintenance
membership lists
men
personal lives
product guides
professional activities
reviews
technical aspects
tributes
women
works
youth

This example is from the *Film Literature Index* thesaurus with a scope note:

tributes [*Use only as a subheading*]

The *scope note* explains how a subject term, or in this case a subheading, should be used (Anderson 1997, 42). Here are examples of general subheadings applied to the subject term *film directors*:

film directors
    personal lives
        Citations: articles on their families, wives, parents, etc.
    professional activities
        Citations: articles on their work, professional associations, union activities, etc.

Here are examples of general subheadings applied to names:

American Society of Cinematographers
    membership lists
Having a Wonderful Crime (d Edward Sutherland 1945 USA)
    technical aspects
Scorsese, Martin
    professional activities
Taylor, Elizabeth
    tributes

Here are examples of subheadings used as unit types:

Cameras
  product guides
    Camcorders. *Consumer Reports* 55:39–41+ [6p] Jun 1990

Provincial, Le (d Gion, Christian 1990 Fr)
  Reviews
    Valot, J. "Le provincial." *Revue du Cinema* Hors series 37:85 1990[1]

Henze, Hans Werner
  works
    [Film music] Hans Werner Henze Filmmusik. T. Nytsch. NZ 167 n3
      May–Jun 2006 p68–9
    [Operas] First nights (Sante Fe Opera's record of promoting new
      works). P. Huscher. Opera (Eng) Festivals Issue 2006 p24–5+[2]

Phillips, Jane
  interviews
    At least equal to heads. J. Parkin. *Times Educ Suppl* no4610 p28 N 19
      2004 (from *Education Index* Feb 2005)

Geographic Subheadings

Geographic subheadings include any place names: continents, countries, states, provinces, cities, towns, lakes, and so on. Subheadings can also be created out of geographic place names which have been standardized. Standardization becomes important because many countries have more than one name. Often there is a formal name and a shorter more popular version. Should the country be called *China* or *The People's Republic of China* in the index? A good source for standardized place names is the LOC Authorities although that format can be cumbersome in a lot of cases. A place name can be standardized without following all the LOC formats, but the indexer must be sure that the internal place name system is consistent within the index itself. An additional subheading for dates of events, or those that indicate the years a country name was used, can be very helpful as well (Anderson 1997, 33).

Here is a subheading format for geographic subheadings:

subject term
  countries
    states or provinces
      cities. date

Here is an example of geographic subheadings with a specific subject term:

film festivals
   United States
      Texas
         Dallas. 2010

Here is an example of dates in the qualifiers of country names:

Germany (until 1949)
Germany (Democratic Republic, 1949–1990)
Germany (Federal Republic, 1949–1990)

Authorized Subject Terms From the Thesaurus

It is also possible to use subject terms from the thesaurus as subheadings. It is not permissible, however, to use a subject term as a subheading that is in any kind of a relationship to the main entry in the thesaurus. See earlier under "Some Rules Governing the Choice of Subject Terms." These rules also apply to subheadings under authorized subject terms.

Subheading Formats in the Index

Subheadings in the index can be formatted as indentions or connected to the subject term by dashes (also called run-in subheadings). The preferred format is indented subheadings unless there is limited space available and then a run-in format will do (Anderson 1997, 30).

Following are an examples of indented subheadings from the *Film Literature Index*:

film industry
   United States
      California
         Los Angeles

periodicals
   academic
      citations
   popular
      citations

The following are examples of subject terms connected to subheadings with dashes (the format of the LOC Authorities):

Children's literature – 19th century – Periodicals
United States – Nevada – Las Vegas – Politics and government

Guidelines for Subject Terms That Always Have the Same Subheadings

A useful way to simplify the indexing of certain similar units is to establish guidelines about the units and format in the index. At the *Film Literature Index*, all conferences, festivals, symposiums, trade fairs, and so on were indexed with specific subject terms and the place and date of the event. This approach also promotes consistency in subject term assignment. Creating guidelines can also apply to unit types or other specific subject entries as well.

Here is an example of guidelines for similar subject terms:

    film festivals
        France
            Cannes. 2013

CONCLUSION

In this chapter, I have taken you on a journey through the processes of periodical indexing. The theoretical concepts that support the different processes of creating periodical indexes came from the impressive article by Susan Klement. Tackling the four most important challenges of periodical indexing took us deeper into the special attributes of periodical indexes: what to index, the importance of the citation, the necessity of a thesaurus, and the aboutness of subject assignment. Finally, I suggested some practical methods for implementing solutions to these challenges and proposed some guidelines to ensure that the thesaurus remains the source of structure for an index. Although there is much, much more that could be said about these topics, our journey has revealed the very heart of the matter of periodical indexing.

ACKNOWLEDGMENTS

I would like to dedicate this chapter to the founders and former managing editors of the *Film Literature Index*, Professors Vincent Aceto and Fred Silva, who provided me with an excellent education in the indexing of periodicals including the importance of high standards for creating an index.

I would especially like to thank two writers who have very generously allowed the use of their articles as readings in my workshop given through Simmons Graduate School of Library and Information Science Continuing Education program. Susan

Klement's wonderful article on the different systems of indexes both confirmed my training in periodical indexing and gave me new ideas about the process. Carolyn Weaver's excellent article on the practical aspects of periodical indexing also supported my beliefs about the differences between book and periodical indexing.

ENDNOTES

1. Examples are all from the *Film Literature Index* v.19, 1991.
2. Both examples from *The Music Index* n.1 2007.

REFERENCES
Periodical Title Abbreviations

A list of the journals online in PubMed through the U.S. National Library of Medicine (which gives title abbreviations as used by PubMed) is available at ftp.ncbi.nih.gov/pubmed/J_Medline.txt.

Journal title abbreviations for science and engineering journals can be found at library.caltech.edu/reference/abbreviations.

More periodical title abbreviations can be found at ISSN International Center at www.issn.org/2-22661-LTWA-online.php.

Periodical Indexing

Alonso-Gamboa, José Octavio, and Jane M. Russell. "Latin American Scholarly Journal Databases: A Look Back to the Way Forward." *ASLIB Proceedings* 64, no. 1(2012): 32–45.

American National Standards Institute/National Information Standards Organization. *Bibliographic References Z39.29-2005*. Bethesda: NISO Press, 2005 – This version of this standard can be downloaded as a PDF free of charge from the website (www.niso.org). There is also a more recent revised version (*Bibliographic References Z39.29-2005 [R2010]*. Bethesda: NISO Press, 2010), which can be purchased through a link on the webpage about this standard.

Anderson, James D. *Guidelines for Indexes and Related Information Retrieval Devices NISO TR02-1997*. Bethesda: NISO Press, 1997 – This technical report can be downloaded as a PDF free of charge from the website (www.niso.org).

Barlow, Caroline. "Serials Indexing: From Journals to Databases." *The Indexer* 27, no. 1(Mar 2009): 2–6.

Beare, Geraldine. *Indexing Newspapers, Magazines and Other Periodicals*. (Occasional Paper 4). London: Society of Indexers, 1999.

Bonura, Larry S. *The Art of Indexing*. New York: Wiley, 1994.

Booth, Pat F. *Indexing: The Manual of Good Practice*. London: K.G. Saur, 2001.

Dunn, Linda, and Deborah Sternklar, eds. *Film Literature Index*. Albany, NY: Film and Television Documentation Center, 1979–2005.

Feather, John, and Paul Sturges, eds. *International Encyclopedia of Information and Library Science*. 2nd ed. London: Routledge, 2003.

Hammer, David. "A Model Retrospective Newspaper Index." *Key Words* 16, no. 3(Jul–Sep 2008): 85–89, 106.

History of Citation Indexing. thomsonreuters.com/productsservices/science/free/essays/history of citation indexing (accessed November 11, 2013).

Hogan, Brian F. "Digital Journal Indexing: Electrified or Electrocuted? Problems, Practicalities and Possibilities: The Case of the CCHA and/et la SCHÉC." *The Indexer* 28, no. 4(Dec 2010): 154–162.

Indexes: A Chapter From the Chicago Manual of Style. 16th ed. Chicago: University of Chicago Press, 2010.

Jacsó, Péter. "The Future of Citation Indexing: An Interview With Eugene Garfield." *Online* 28, no. 1(Jan–Feb 2004): 38–40. Available from www2.hawaii.edu/~jacso/extra/egyeb/gene-interview.pdf (accessed November 11, 2013).

Klement, Susan. "Open-System Versus Closed-System Indexing: A Vital Distinction." *The Indexer* 23, no. 1(Apr 2002): 23–31.

Lancaster, F. W. *Indexing and Abstracting in Theory and Practice*. 3rd ed. Champaign: University of Illinois Graduate School of Library and Information Science/Facet Publishing, 2003.

Mulvany, Nancy C. *Indexing Books*. Chicago: University of Chicago Press, 1994.

Olson, Debbie. "Volunteer Indexing Projects: Gaining Experience While Providing a Service in Your Community." *Key Words* 15, no. 2(Apr–Jun 2007): 46.

Reeder, Josh. *Indexing Genealogy Publications*. Damascus, MD: R.D. Earnest Associates, 1994.

Russell, Mary. "Tips and Hints: Annual Journal Indexes." *ANZSI Newsletter* 4, no. 5(Jun 2008): 4. Available from www.anzsi.org/site/newsletters2008.asp (accessed November 11, 2013).

Soper, Mary Ellen, Larry N. Osborne, and Douglas L. Zweizig. *The Librarian's Thesaurus: A Concise Guide to Library and Information Terms*. Chicago: American Library Association, 1990.

Thomas, Judy. "The VIC in July: Indexing The Argus." *ANZSI Newsletter* 6, no. 8(Sep 2010): 5. Available fromwww.anzsi.org/site/newsletters2010.asp (accessed November 11, 2013).

Walker, Mary A., and Elizabeth C. McKoo. "Evolution of a State Periodical Index: Converting an In-House Index to a MARC-Based Database on the Web." *The Serials Librarian* 55, no. 1–2(2008): 184–209.

Weaver, Carolyn. "The Gist of Journal Indexing." *Key Words* 10, no. 1(Jan–Feb 2002): 6–22.

Weaver, Carolyn. "The Indexer as Consultant: Collaborative Indexing of Community Newspapers." *Key Words* 14, no. 1(Jan–Feb 2006): 18–23, 33. Available from www.asindexing.org/i4a/pages/index.cfm?pageid=3415 (accessed November 11, 2013).

Wellisch, Hans H. "Book and Periodical Indexing." *Journal of the American Society for Information Science* 45, no. 8(1994): 620–627.

Wellisch, Hans H. *Glossary of Terminology in Abstracting, Classification, Indexing and Thesaurus Construction.* 2nd ed. Medford, NJ: Information Today, Inc., 2000.

Wellisch, Hans H. *Indexing From A to Z.* 2nd ed. New York: H.W. Wilson Co., 1995.

Controlled Vocabularies and Thesauri

American National Standards Institute/National Information Standards Organization. *Guidelines for the Construction, Format, and Management of Monolingual Controlled Vocabularies Z39.19-2005.* Bethesda: NISO Press, 2005 – This version of this standard can be downloaded as a PDF free of charge from the website (www.niso.org). There is also a more recent revised version (*Guidelines for the Construction, Format, and Management of Monolingual Controlled Vocabularies ANSI/NISO Z39.19 [R2010].* Bethesda: NISO Press, 2010; Related international standard: ISO 2788), which can be purchased through a link on the webpage about this standard.

Coyle, Karen. "Vocabularies: Term Lists and Thesauri." *Library Technology Reports* 48, no. 4(May–Jun 2012): 27–35.

Fayen, Emily. "A New Standard for Controlled Vocabularies." *The Indexer* 24, no. 2(Oct 2004): 62–65. Available from www.theindexer.org/index.php?option=comcontent&task=view&id=95&Itemid=60 (accessed November 11, 2013).

Library of Congress. *Authorities.* authorities.loc.gov (accessed November 11, 2013).

Marshall, Julia. "Controlled Vocabularies: A Primer." *Key Words* 13, no. 4(Oct–Dec 2005): 120–124.

Marshall, Julia. "Controlled Vocabulary: Implementation and Evaluation." *Key Words* 14, no. 1(Apr–Jun 2006): 53–57, 59.

Miller, Joseph, and Patricia Kuhr. "LCSH and Periodical Indexing: Adoption vs. Adaptation." *Cataloging & Classification Quarterly* 29, no. 1–2(2000): 159–168.

Chapter 11

Chinese Personal Names: How to Decode Them

Lai Heung Lam © 2014

Author's Note: All family names in this article are in capital letters for clarity.

Chinese names are puzzles to Westerners who do not know much about Chinese culture or language. Librarian Junlin PAN illustrates this fact with an interesting story of her constant struggles to get her name right while living and working in the U.S.[1] Indeed, the Romanized forms of Chinese names are often the cause of frustration to catalogers, indexers, and those who have to decode them for work or business. Name order probably poses the greatest challenge as it is sometimes impossible to determine unless you know the person. This problem is aggravated by the fact that publishers often have varying rules with name formats, thereby creating inconsistencies and confusion.

To understand the complexities of Romanized Chinese names, it is important to know some basic facts about Chinese name formats. There are two forms of written scripts in the Chinese language: traditional and simplified. The traditional form is used in Taiwan, Hong Kong, Macau, and many of the old diasporic Chinese communities, whereas the simplified form prevails in mainland China, Singapore, Malaysia, and the rest of the world. In terms of pronunciation, Chinese is a monosyllabic language (i.e., one character is pronounced as one syllable). When written in Chinese scripts, Chinese names always follow the format of family name first, then given name. Many Westerners confuse the middle syllable of a three-character Chinese name as a middle name, but Chinese do not have any middle name convention. This misunderstanding often occurs when names are written in three parts, as often is the case for Hong Kong, Singaporean, and Malaysian Chinese names.

Most Chinese have three-character names that are Romanized in different ways depending on where they live and sometimes the dialects they speak. The two main Romanization systems in use today are *Hanyu pinyin*, or *pinyin* for short, and *Wade-Giles*, both based on Mandarin pronunciation. Except in rare cases as with minority groups, names of mainland Chinese always follow the pinyin format. Pinyin names have two parts: family name first, then given name as one word, such as MAO Zedong or YAO Ming. Let us take a look at the four Chinese name formats with examples of well-known people, all rendered in pinyin:

1. Three-character names = 1-character family name (FN) + 2-character given name (GN)
Example: MAO Zedong (former political leader in China)
Three-character names are the most common format of all Chinese names.

	FN	GN	GN
Name in simplified script	□ +	泽	东
Pronounced in Mandarin as	MAO	Ze	Dong
Full pinyin form	MÁO Zédōng		
Full Wade-Giles form	MAO² Tse²-tung¹		

2. Two-character names = 1-character family name (FN) + 1-character given name (GN)
Example: YAO Ming (Chinese basketball player)
The problem with this format is that it creates uncertainties as to which part of the name is the family name. Many Westerners have difficulties in determining whether the name Yao Ming is family name first as in YAO Ming or family name last as in Yao MING.

	FN	GN
Name in simplified script	□ +	明
Pronounced in Mandarin as	YAO	Ming
Full pinyin form	YÁO Míng	
Full Wade-Giles form	YAO² Ming²	

3. Four-character names = 2-character family name (FN) + 2-character given name (GN)

Example: SIMA Xiangru (scholar of the Han Dynasty)

A minority of the Chinese population also has two-character compound family names, so some names can be four characters long.

	FN	FN	GN	GN
Name in simplified script	☐	☐ + 相	如	
Pronounced in Mandarin as	SI	MA	Xiang	Ru
Full pinyin form	SĪMǍ Xiāngrú			
Full Wade-Giles form	SSU^1-MA^3 Hsiang^1-ju^2			

4. Three-character names = 2-character family name (FN) + 1-character given name (GN)

Example: ZHUGE Liang - chancellor of the Three Kingdoms period

This format causes the most confusion as it looks like the last part is the family name but in actual fact, the first two characters form part of a compound family name.

	FN	FN	GN
Name in simplified script	☐	☐ + 亮	
Pronounced in Mandarin as	ZHU	GE	Liang
Full pinyin form	ZHŪGĚ Liàng		
Full Wade-Giles form	CHU^1-KO^3 Liang^4		

COMPLEXITIES OF ROMANIZED CHINESE NAMES

As can be seen from the examples just given, it is easy to imagine the difficulties in identifying the cut-off point between family and given names. This also explains why knowing the order does not always guarantee success in identifying which part of a name forms the family name and which part the given name. In addition to name order, there are other complexities as well. The following sections caution indexers when working with Romanized Chinese names.

Name Order

Written in logographic scripts, Chinese names are simple and straightforward. They can only appear in one order: always family name first, then given name. Nobody would ever change it to any other way. Name order becomes a problem only when Chinese names are Romanized. Imagine trying to decode names like Linda Miranda or George Thomas if you do not know the order, unless of course there is a comma in between to indicate otherwise. If you believe a name to be in pinyin form, you can be sure that it is family name first, except when someone inverts it deliberately to make things "easier" for Westerners. Junlin PAN, mentioned earlier, is one such example where she reversed her original name order to fit in with American name conventions. Because pinyin names are always family name first, most indexers treat them as they are printed; no comma follows Chinese family names in indexes as they do other types of names.

However, Chinese names also come in other Romanized forms apart from pinyin and may not always be family name first. This is why name order causes so much confusion, particularly for an international audience. In recent years, many librarians and politicians from Hong Kong and Japan have started to capitalize their family names on official documents and websites to avoid confusion. The U.S. Central Intelligence Agency's online World Leaders directory also displays family names of world leaders in capitalized form for the sake of clarity, making it easier for those who have to work with politicians' names. Unfortunately, practices like these are not as widespread as we would like.

It is interesting to note that many overseas Chinese during the gold-mining era of the 19th and early 20th century had their names permanently reversed in English, often by immigration officials. The SEW HOY family in New Zealand is one such example where CHOIE Sew Hoy's given name, Sew Hoy, became his family name. However, this name reversal was not just for him, but for all descendants after him too.[2] Many Chinese names from that period were also deliberately anglicized by immigration officials—family names like LO or LAW became LOWE, SHAO became SHAW, and LUI became LOUIE.

Different Romanization Systems in Use Simultaneously

Since pinyin became an international standard in 1979, all mainland Chinese names are Romanized in this format. However, people outside mainland China still continue using other conventions as they have for decades. An atypical example is the former Chinese National Party leader CHIANG Kai Shek. His name appears in different forms depending on where and which Romanization system is used:

Romanized Form	Romanization System	Spelling Based on
JIANG Jieshi	Pinyin	Mandarin (mainland China)
CHIANG Chieh-shih	Wade-Giles	Mandarin (Taiwan)
CHIANG Kai-shek	Wade-Giles	Cantonese (Western world)

According to pinyin, JIANG Jieshi is the standard form, and this is how all Mandarin speakers pronounce his name. But unlike MAO Zedong, whose name had a quick and easy transition from its former Wade-Giles form of MAO Tse-tung, CHIANG Kai Shek, based on Cantonese dialectal pronunciation, remains the more popular form to this day. This is rather a rare example for well-known figures but demonstrates a typical confusion because JIANG Jieshi, CHIANG Kai Shek, and CHIANG Chieh-shih all sound very different from each other.

In Taiwan, even though the government made pinyin official in 2009, people still observe the Wade-Giles rules, which have been used for decades.[3] The Wade-Giles system employs a lot of diacritic marks, as well as superscript numbers, to indicate levels of tone in each syllable. Wade-Giles names also have hyphens in between two-syllable given names, making Romanized Taiwanese names easy to identify.

In Hong Kong where Cantonese is spoken, the government uses its own rules based on the *Jyutping* system to Romanize personal names. However, people can still determine how they want to spell their names. This lack of standardization is mainly because there is no internationally recognized system for the Cantonese dialect. Many authors and family history researchers also use the *Yale* or *Sidney Lau* systems to Romanize Cantonese names. A distinct feature of Romanized Hong Kong Chinese names is that each syllable is written separately. They are neither joined together as in pinyin names nor separated with a hyphen like the Wade-Giles format. The same is true of Singaporean and Malaysian Chinese names. Hong Kong businessman LI Ka Shing and former Singaporean Prime Minister LEE Kuan Yew are two such examples.

For the rest of the older diasporic Chinese communities, there is hardly any standard at all. Most people use self-deduced ways to Romanize names based on their spoken dialect, giving many idiosyncratic systems. This explains why there are so many different spellings of the same family names for many overseas Chinese.

Omission of Tone Marks, Diacritic Marks, and Apostrophes

Correct use of the pinyin and Wade-Giles systems very much depends on tone marks, in pinyin as diacritic marks and in Wade-Giles as superscript numbers.

However, Romanized Chinese names are rarely written with these marks because they look cumbersome and add complexities when entering into computers. Wade-Giles names in their correct form also make abundant use of the diacritic mark *ayn* (often written as an apostrophe to indicate aspiration), which easily confuses people. Designed for academics and specialists, the Wade-Giles system has been heavily criticized as being inaccurate in terms of Chinese pronunciation, mainly because most people do not know how it works. As such, authors and editors often leave those marks out altogether, causing a lot of confusion for the "educated" reader. A classic example is the martial art term *T'ai Chi*. The ayn after T indicates an aspirated sound (i.e., with a puff of air when you say the word). Without the ayn, T is pronounced as D, so Tai is then actually pronounced as Dai. As for Chi, because it is written without the ayn, it is non-aspirated (i.e., with no puff of air when you say it), so it is pronounced as Ji. The following shows how ayns work in terms of pronouncing T'ai Chi in Wade Giles, and its pinyin equivalent:

	Romanized as	Pronounced as
In pinyin	Taiji	Tai Ji
In Wade-Giles (without the ayn mark)	Tai Chi	Dai Ji
In Wade-Giles (with the ayn mark)	T'ai Chi	Tai Ji

The irony with Wade-Giles is that both the presence and absence of ayns confuse people. Despite this, it is worth knowing that this diacritic mark is an important part of the Wade-Giles system and as such warrants careful treatment.

For pinyin names, the absence of umlauts also creates confusion. Without this diacritic mark, u can be pronounced in two ways, either as u or ü. In pinyin, ju, qu and xu are always pronounced as jü, qü and xü so there are no ambiguities. However lu and lü (both are family names) represent completely different characters and need to be sorted separately in indexes. Similarly, nu and nü are two different words too. On the other hand, apostrophes are also an important element in pinyin names as they separate joined syllables in the case where there may be confusion. For example, WANG Yan'an is pronounced as WANG Yan An but without the apostrophe, it can also be pronounced as WANG Ya Nan, two completely different names.

Dialectal Variations

China has seven major dialect groups and hundreds of sub-dialects that are mutually unintelligible. As can be seen in CHIANG Kai Shek's example, dialectal variations (variations in spelling) play an important part in how Chinese names appear in their Romanized forms. A majority of the international Chinese diasporic communities is from Southern China where the Guangzhou (Cantonese), Kejia (Hakka), and Fujian (Hokkien) dialects are spoken. Consequently, many overseas Chinese have strange-looking Romanized names because of uncommon dialectal pronunciations. Other names look odd because people did not follow common conventions and came up with their own idiosyncratic spellings. The family name Huang (in Mandarin pinyin) can be Romanized as follows depending on the dialect:

Dialect	Romanized Form
Mandarin	Huang, Hwang
Guangzhou (Cantonese)	Wong
Kejia (Hakka)	Bong
Fujian (Hokkien)	Oei, Oi, Ooi, Uy, Wee
Chaozhou (Chiu Chow/ Teochew)	Ng, Ong

One Name Shared by Many People

Similar to the English versions of John Smith or Mary Jones, the overuse of a small pool of Chinese family names means that there is a large number of Chinese sharing exactly the same names. In addition to this, there is also the problem of people having different names, but when Romanized they all become spelled the same! This coincidence is due to the large number of homophones in the Chinese language. A comparable example in English is the name Mary Ann, which can also be spelled as Maryanne, Marianne, or Maryann—all having the same pronunciation but different spellings. Similarly, Chinese names that are different but share the same sounds can only be distinguished by their written characters.

The omission of tone marks in Romanized Chinese names creates further problems. Chinese is a tonal language; Mandarin has four tones while Cantonese has nine. Tone marks in Romanized names provide vital information because they help differentiate characters that have the same sounds but different tones. In Mandarin, the syllable *yi* can be pronounced in four different tones as follows:

Four Tones of *yi*	Tone Level
yī	high
yí	rising
yǐ	falling then rising
yì	falling

The fourth falling tone *yì* alone represents 80 different characters in an everyday use Chinese dictionary! Tones are indicated in pinyin with diacritic marks and in Wade-Giles as superscript numbers (although rarely used). The name of SIMA Qian, the father of Chinese historiography, can be written with tone marks as follows:

In pinyin	SĪMǍ Qiān
In Wade-Giles	SSU[1]-MA[3] Ch'ien[1]

The following example shows six different persons all sharing the same pinyin name WANG Wei. Without tone marks, the names are all spelled exactly the same. But even when written with tone marks, the last two pairs still cause confusion:

王韦 WANG Wéi

王違 WANG Wéi

王緯 WANG Wěi

王瑋 WANG Wěi

王巍 WANG Wēi

王薇 WANG Wēi

Name duplication has become a huge problem, particularly within the biomedical and science publishing field because more and more Chinese authors are publishing their work internationally. Some even went as far as to describe this confusion as an identity crisis for Chinese authors.[4] In works of classical Chinese literature and philosophy, name duplication frequently happens. This is why in many authoritative works where names are important and numerous, authors or editors usually list corresponding Chinese characters next to the Romanized version for easy reference as well as name disambiguation. However, this may prove impractical because publishers may not be willing to include Chinese scripts, or authors and editors do not know the Chinese language. Sometimes the only way to solve name duplication problems in indexes is to include birth and death dates, or add attributes such as the individual's profession to provide differentiation.

Female Married Names

It is very rare for Chinese women to alter their names after marriage. However, many female politicians, members of the Hong Kong's upper class, and some Taiwanese do add their husbands' names in front of their maiden names. Married names are similar to how compound family names work when written in Chinese. The name of Madame CHIANG Kai Shek whose maiden name is SOONG May-ling (also SUNG Mei-ling) can be written as:

Madame CHIANG SOONG May-ling, or
Madame CHIANG Kai Shek,
but **NOT** Madame CHIANG May-ling

Adoption of Western Names

The adoption of Western names explains why some Chinese have more than one name and why name order can sometimes become a nightmare to decode. Either as birth names or in addition to the given name, many Chinese in Hong Kong, Singapore, and Malaysia adopt Western names. The standard format used by the English press in Hong Kong actually has the family name in the middle! It places the adopted Western name first, then family name, and lastly a hyphenated two-syllable given name. The name of the former Chief Executive of the Hong Kong Government appears in Hong Kong's English press as:

Donald TSANG Yam-kuen

Former Singaporean Prime Minister LEE Kuan Yew also has an English name in addition to his Chinese one: Harry.[5] His full name can be written in a variety of ways:

LEE Kuan Yew, Harry
Kuan Yew LEE, Harry
Harry LEE Kuan Yew
Harry Kuan Yew LEE, or
Harry LEE

If we add initialization and hyphenation to the names above, the list will go on and on. Complexities like these may help to explain why many overseas Chinese simply drop their Chinese given names for the sake of convenience; Harry LEE is definitely a lot easier for Westerners to remember than LEE Kuan Yew.

Ethnic Minority Names

China has 55 minority groups, each with completely different naming conventions from the Chinese Han people. One example is Tibetan names. Names of the Tibetan people are often Romanized into pinyin based on the sound of the Tibetan words—a practice known within the scholarly community as *ethnic pinyin*. However, there also exists another way of Romanization that is a pinyin version of the Chinese characters transcribed from the original Tibetan name. As a result, multiple versions of the same name may occur.[6] In view of this arbitrary practice, minority names should be treated differently from pinyin names.

Names Written in Chinese Scripts Do Not Always Belong to Chinese

This is probably the least expected of all possible confusions. The languages of the Sinosphere (Chinese cultural sphere) countries—China, Japan, and Korea—are different, but all three countries use logographic Chinese characters, known as *hanzi* in Chinese, *kanji* in Japanese, and *hanja* in Korean. Written in Chinese scripts, Chinese and Korean names can sometimes be hard to distinguish, both countries employing three-character names as the most common format. Some Japanese also have three-character names but they are relatively rare. When I studied in Japan, I was able to continue using my written name in Chinese. However, the three characters of my name were pronounced in completely different ways: My Japanese teacher and friends would pronounce it based on Sino-Japanese pronunciation, and my Korean classmates the Sino-Korean way. What is more, I also happened to share the same name with some Japanese women, and they would pronounce it according to Japanese pronunciation. Thus my name can be Romanized within the Sinosphere in five different ways:

My name in traditional Chinese script	林麗香
Pronounced in	**Romanized as**
Cantonese	LAM Lai Heung
Mandarin pinyin	LIN Lixiang
Sino-Japanese	LIN Reika
Sino-Korean (Revised Romanization)	IM Ryeo-hyang
Japanese (Hepburn Romanization)	HAYASHI Reika

Sometimes There Is No Rule At All

Outside China, there are often no strict requirements as to how people Romanize their names so formats can be unpredictable. My sister and her husband (who live in Cantonese-speaking Hong Kong) Romanized the names of their children as CHENG Log G and CHENG Log C, both very unusual spelling for the Chinese. The G and C are not initials but were chosen because these two letters replicate almost the exact same sounds in Cantonese. Names such as these easily confuse Chinese as much as they do Westerners!

TIPS AND SUGGESTIONS

It helps to know that decoding Chinese personal names may not always be as complicated as suggested above. No doubt it is a lot easier if you only need to work with pinyin names. For those who are less fortunate, here are a few tips and suggestions to help you avoid getting confused:

- Except in rare cases, all pinyin names are family name first followed by given name. The same is true of Singaporean and Malaysian Chinese names. Hong Kong and Taiwanese names can be tricky as people sometimes invert their names to fit in with Western standards.

- Be cautious of names on book covers if they are works by Western and Chinese co-authors. These names often appear alongside each other in "mixed-orders": Western author names are arranged family name last while Chinese author names the opposite. Imagine a work co-authored by LEE Kuan Yew and Barack OBAMA. One would readily assume Yew as the family name, but in this instance it is obvious that it is LEE and not Yew. This inconsistent practice leads to a lot of name order confusion.

- Take extra care not to miss diacritic marks and apostrophes in both Wade-Giles and pinyin names if they have been rendered properly.

- Most Taiwanese names are still in Wade-Giles format and can be easy to identify. Pinyin and Wade-Giles names have different starting and ending syllable combinations shown as follows:

	Pinyin	Wade-Giles
Starting syllables	B-, D-, G-, Q-, X-, Z-	Hs-, Ts-
Ending syllables	-an, -ian, -ong, -ue, -ie	-ung, -ueh, -ieh
Example	MAO Zedong	MAO Tse-tung

- Watch out for names from Hong Kong, Singapore, and Malaysia, particularly those with adopted Western names, as the family name may sometimes be embedded in the middle. Names from these regions almost always have spaces between each syllable as in LEE Kuan Yew. The same is true of most overseas Chinese names.

- It is important to know that names commonly used may not be the person's "real" name. For example, SUN Yat-sen's name is his pseudonym, and he has many other names. He is known to all Chinese as SUN Zhongshan, which is actually his Japanese name. CHIANG Kai Shek is known in Taiwan under his official name CHIANG Chung-cheng. Chinese literary authors, artists, calligraphers, and painters also tend to have many different pseudonyms or style names. It is always a good practice to add *See* references or create double entries so people can find those variant names.

- If you are sure a married woman uses her husband's name in addition to her maiden name, the name can be indexed in several ways. Again, it is helpful to add a cross-reference or create a double entry for the maiden name. For example:

CHIANG SOONG May-ling [similar to a compound family name], or CHIANG May-ling (SOONG) [maiden name in parentheses]

- Do not attempt to translate Wade-Giles name formats into pinyin and vice versa without reference to the actual Chinese scripts. In some cases, these two systems do not correspond to each other. For example, although ch- or ch'- in Wade-Giles can still be ch- when translated into pinyin, it can also be j-, q-, or zh-.

- If a name appears in Wade-Giles form and you are aware of the correct pinyin version, it would be helpful for readers to include the pinyin name in brackets or create a *See* reference entry:

Chiang Kai Shek. *See* Jiang Jieshi

- With works that involve a lot of names, it is worth finding out if publishers are willing to include a separate name index as it is a lot easier for readers.

If you find yourself constantly struggling with name order, Liqun DAI wrote an article, "Hundred Surname Pinyin Index," that can help you decode name order for pinyin names.[7] For non-pinyin names, extra research is often needed to ensure accuracy. However, there are times when it is just impossible to identify which part of a name is the family name. For instance, all three characters of my name, when Romanized, can be family names. The same is true of my husband's and my daughter's names. In such cases you have to seek advice from the author or editor. The good news for indexers is that a lot of the detective work would have already been done with names decoded when the work arrives in your hands. It is also common for authors to include introductory notes indicating how they choose to Romanize Chinese names within their works. Authors sometimes have bilingual glossaries which can be helpful for indexers as reference materials, even though you can only guess from the look of the Chinese scripts if you do not know the language.

For those having to work with ancient materials such as classical Chinese literature or historical works about imperial China, it can be very challenging as name duplication is common. Taiwanese authors living abroad or Chinese scholars in Taiwan who publish in the English language may still use a lot of Wade-Giles names, often alongside pinyin equivalents. This practice is particularly common in works such as Chinese martial arts. With jobs like these, names can be tedious to work with because of the abundant use of ayns and other diacritic marks. It may also involve a lot of background research and communicating with either the author or editor to get things right. In such cases, you may seek help by networking with other Chinese-speaking indexers as they can answer questions you may have when you get into tangles.

FINAL COMMENTS

Lastly, it is worth mentioning that pinyin was not designed as a Romanization system for foreigners, but as a teaching aid for the Chinese people and has been used in mainland China since 1958. It was not until 1979 that it came into widespread use internationally as a Romanization system for non-Chinese. Another interesting concept put forth by Yewang WANG is that a person's Romanized name is a phonetic version of his original name written in English form. It is not a real English name, but rather a "surrogate" name.[8] Understanding this concept may help indexers appreciate why Chinese names can be Romanized in so many different ways.

For those interested in finding out more about issues with Romanized Chinese names, there is a resource section at the end of this article. The Library of Congress Authorities and the Virtual International Authority File Databases are both very helpful tools for indexers when working with established Chinese names. There are also plenty of resources on the internet. Wikipedia has a wealth of information on naming conventions, not only about Chinese names but names of all kinds, with some very interesting debates on template rules too. Last but not least, veteran indexer Noeline Bridge's "Resources for Personal Names" provides invaluable guidance for indexers who need to locate resources when decoding personal names of all kinds, not just Chinese. It is certainly an important resource not to be missed.[9] Good luck and happy indexing Chinese names!

The author welcomes any questions or comments on this article and can be reached at laihlam.hk@gmail.com.

ENDNOTES

1. Pan Junlin, "On Your Name and My Name: Transliteration of Chinese Personal Names," 2003, accessed October 11, 2013, www.white-clouds.com/iclc/cliej/cl16 pan.htm.

2. James Ng, "Sew Hoy, Charles," *Dictionary of New Zealand Biography Te Ara – The Encyclopedia of New Zealand*, accessed October 11, 2013, www.teara.govt.nz/en/ biographies/2s14/1.

3. Shih Hsiu-chuan, "Hanyu Pinyin to Be Standard System in 2009," *Taipei Times*, September 18, 2008, accessed October 11, 2013, www.taipeitimes.com/News/taiwan/ archives/2008/09/18/2003423528.

4. Jane Qiu, "Scientific Publishing: Identity Crisis," *Nature* 451 (February 13, 2008): 766–67, www.nature.com/news/2008/080213/full/451766a.html (accessed October 11, 2013).

5. Terry McCarthy, "Lee Kuan Yew," *Time World*, August 23, 1999, www.time.com/time/ world/article/0,8599,2054444,00.html (accessed October 11, 2013).

6. Tibetan and Himalayan Library, "Ethnic Pinyin Transcription of Tibetan," 2012, accessed October 11, 2013, collab.itc.virginia.edu/wiki/tibetan-script/Ethnic%20Pinyin %20of%20Tibetan.html.

7. Dai Liqun, "The Hundred Surnames: A Pinyin Index," *The Indexer* 25, no. 2 (2006.): C3–8.

8. Wang Yewang, "A Look Into Chinese Persons' Names in Bibliography Practice," *Cataloging & Classification Quarterly* 31, no.1 (2000): 51–81.

9. Noeline Bridge, "Resources for Personal Names," in *Indexing Names*, ed. Noeline Bridge (Medford, NJ: Information Today, Inc., 2012), 339–352.

RESOURCES

Central Intelligence Agency. "World Leaders." 2013. https://www.cia.gov/library/publications/ world-leaders-1/index.html.

China Vitae. www.chinavitae.com.

Dai Liqun. "Chinese Personal Names." *The Indexer* 25, no. 2 (2006): C1–2.

——. "The Hundred Surnames: A Pinyin Index." *The Indexer* 25, no. 2 (2006): C3–8.

Harrison, Scott Edward. "Chinese Names in English." *Cataloging & Classification Quarterly* 15 no. 2 (1992): 3–14.

Hong Kong Chinese Authority (Name). www.julac.org/hkcan.

Hu Qianli. "How to Distinguish and Catalog Chinese Personal Names." *Cataloging & Classification Quarterly* 19, no. 1 (1994): 29–60.

Interpol. *A Guide to Names and Naming Practice*. March 2006. www.mountainrecce.com/ INT%20NAMING%20PRACTICES%20guide2006.pdf.

Lam Lai Heung. "Chinese, Japanese and Korean (CJK) Names: Resources for the Indexer." *The Indexer* 31, no. 2 (2013): C1–6.

Library of Congress Authorities. authorities.loc.gov.

Library of Congress. "Library of Congress Pinyin Conversion Project: New Chinese Romanization Guidelines. www.loc.gov/catdir/pinyin/romcover.html.

Library of Congress. "Library of Congress Pinyin Conversion Project – Frequently Asked Questions: What's the Difference Between Wade-Giles and Pinyin?" www.loc.gov/catdir/ pinyin/difference.html.

Lin, Joseph C. "Chinese Names Containing a Non-Chinese Name. *Cataloging & Classification Quarterly* 9, no. 1 (1988): 69–81.

Pinyin.info: A Guide to the Writing of Mandarin Chinese in Romanization. pinyin.info.

Sun, Xiao-Ling. "English Versions of Chinese Authors' Names in Biomedical Journals: Observations and Recommendations. *Science Editor* 25, no. 1 (2002): 3–4.

Tan, Peter K. W. "Englishised Names?" *English Today* 17 (2001): 45–53.

Taylor, Insup, and Martin M. Taylor. *Writing and Literacy in Chinese, Korean and Japanese*. Amsterdam, Philadelphia: John Benjamins Publishing, 1995.

VIAF: The Virtual International Authority File. viaf.org.

Wang Yewang. "A Look Into Chinese Persons' Names in Bibliography Practice." *Cataloging & Classification Quarterly* 31, no. 1 (2000): 51–81.

Chapter 12

The Logic and Language of Patterns

Scott Smiley © 2014

You are working on an index in the indexing software of your choice, and you have a whole list of subheadings that begin with "and." You have decided that you want to move all of these "ands" to the end of the subheadings, but the task of changing hundreds of such entries is daunting. Patterns to the rescue! In a situation like this, patterns make the job much easier by enabling you to change all of those records at once.

One note about using this chapter to learn how to use patterns: I suggest you read this with a blank card or folded paper with you, to block out the answers whenever I pose a problem. You will learn best if you stop to figure out how to formulate the problem or create the pattern yourself, before reading on to the pattern as I have given it. Since learning patterns can be complicated, don't feel that you need to read this entire chapter at once. Master each concept before moving onto the next.

WHAT ARE PATTERNS?

Patterns (also called *pattern matching*, *wildcard find and replace*, or *advanced search and replace*) are common to many software programs, not just indexing software. Microsoft Word, for example, also uses these (called find and replace using wildcards). For us indexers, they offer a powerful tool to save time with indexing software, and they can be used in CINDEX, MACREX, and SKY Index. Patterns use special symbols to allow you to find or find and replace something that fits a certain shape.

By fitting a certain *shape*, I mean, for example, any main heading beginning with a capital letter, or any subheading that has text in parentheses, or any heading that has a four-digit number in parentheses (a year), and so on. And then, with replace, you can manipulate it: For example, move "and" at the beginning of a subheading to the end, or make all acronyms in parentheses trade places with the spelled out text. The possibilities are endless, and using patterns can save a lot of time by not making you go in and change a whole bunch of records one at a time. The purpose of this chapter is to explain the process of formulating and using patterns. My intent here is not to give you a list of patterns that you can use but won't understand; rather I attempt to demystify patterns so that you can create them when you need them. The *logic* of patterns is how to formulate a problem into something that can be used as a pattern; the *language* of patterns is the set of symbols that software programs use to communicate what you want the software to do.

MACROS VS. PATTERNS

I want to make a distinction between patterns and macros, which is another time-saving device that can help you avoid doing the same thing over and over to many index entries. Whereas patterns use a particular shape that you define for the computer to find or find and replace something, macros are not based on find and replace. Macros are based on a series of *actions* that are recorded and saved so you can repeat them. Some things are better done with one or the other, and some things can be done with either. Macros are not covered in this chapter.

One particularity about patterns is that when replacing, you can only replace something within one field. You can specify any field (e.g., main heading, subheading, locator field) or let it match any field. But you cannot typically move something from the subheading to the main heading, for example (at least not directly; later in the chapter is an example that gets around this issue). If you need to move things between fields, then you might be able to use a macro for that instead.

FINDING EXACTLY WHAT YOU WANT

Since patterns are based on find and replace, I'm going to use a couple of analogies to illustrate the idea of narrowing down what you are *finding* to exactly what you want, with whatever variations. The first illustration is the self-checkout at the grocery store; have you ever used these? (If you have long harbored a hatred of self-checkouts and go to great lengths to avoid them, then please feel free to skip this illustration!) Suppose you have a bag of Fuji apples you are buying, and you need to communicate what you have to the store's computer. In essence, you need to *match* to the Fuji apples. There are a number of ways you can do this, including punching in the numeric code that stands for Fuji apples. But if you don't have the little stickers that say the code, you can go about another process of narrowing down to get down to exactly what you want to match. In my local store, I can choose Select by Picture (yay—no numbers!). Here is what happens: I hit the Select by Picture button and am presented with a series of choices that narrow the possibilities down to what I'm trying to match. First I choose Fruits, and then Apples, and finally Fuji. So I have narrowed down the gazillions of things that are in the store to exactly what I'm buying: Fuji apples.

THE HIGH SCHOOL KID FROM MARS

When you are working with patterns, you have to use precise language that the software will understand. I think of the software as a high school kid from Mars whom you've hired for the summer to help you with some indexing tasks. She will do *exactly* what you tell her, but her vocabulary is limited so you have to work within her language. And you want to watch her to be sure that what you told her is really what you wanted her to do. This is an indexing program using patterns: limited vocabulary, good at following directions in its own language.

So, for example, using our "and" example from earlier, if you told your high school kid from Mars to "take any 'and' at the beginning of a subheading and move it to the end," she would just give you a confused look. "Take" and "move" are not in her vocabulary—she thinks in terms of find and replace (or "change to") instead. So you need to phrase what you want as "find something that looks like *this* and change it to *this*."

I like to approach this issue by first getting down in English exactly what is needed, then translating that problem into the find-and-replace system of the software (still in English, but using the limited vocabulary of the high school kid from Mars), and then finally translating that into the symbols for the program.

MOVING THE FRUIT AROUND

To inch toward that Martian vocabulary, and to illustrate the kinds of things that patterns can do, I want to use pieces of fruit. We'll use the pieces of fruit to stand for something, which is how CINDEX, MACREX, and SKY use the pattern symbols. So an apple stands for "something," a banana stands for "something else," and a pear stands for "something else indeed"—three different pieces of a main heading, for example. You can ask your software to look for any main headings that match the following shape (imagine these as the pictures of each fruit, rather than the spelled-out words for them):

> *find:*   apple + banana + pear

and then you can manipulate them. You could replace this shape with:

> *replace with:*   apple + banana

(Here you have deleted the pear, but your Martian doesn't know that—all she knows is that you have replaced apple + banana + pear with apple + banana.)

Or instead of deleting, you could add:

find:	apple + banana + pear
replace with:	apple + banana + pear + orange

Or rearrange them:

find:	apple + banana + pear
replace with:	pear + banana + apple

All this is being done within the Martian language of "find this, replace it with that." The key, when using patterns, is that you need to identify the unique shape of what you are looking for, to distinguish it from everything else in your index. In other words, define your apples, and so on. Figuring this out is where we use the process of:

- Explain in English

- Explain in Martian

- Translate to symbols

WILDCARDS: THE "SOMEBODY"

Like the fruit in the earlier examples, the symbols you will be using *stand for* something. This can be called the "Somebody." You might be looking for Somebody at the beginning of the subheading, or Somebody inside parentheses, or Somebody who looks like a year (four-digit number). We're going to gradually build up the possibilities of what these things can stand for, starting with the simplest.

Any Character

This simplest piece is a wildcard that *stands for* "any character." The idea is to use the flexibility of the symbols to allow you to find anything that matches a shape, rather than having to type in the exact characters. In CINDEX 2, MACREX, and SKY, this "any character" symbol is the question mark, and in CINDEX 3 it is a period. Since the question mark is more common, I'll use that in the illustrations here. (Since the symbolism of the various programs are similar, for the rest of this chapter I will primarily use the CINDEX 2 patterns, for simplicity. You can see the equivalents for other software in Tables 12.1, 12.2, and 12.3 at the end of the chapter. My emphasis here is on the *logic,* which applies to all.)

If you simply search for "?" (ticking the Patterns checkbox, so your software knows you're using symbols rather than looking for an actual question mark—always do this when using special pattern symbols), what will you get? The results will be any entry that has any character—usually all the entries in the index. But suppose I want to find all entries that have no subheadings? That is the English question. If I explain that in Martian it is: "find all entries that do not have any character in the subheading field." And finally, let's translate to symbols. First we tick the Pattern or Pattern Matching box to tell the software "Alert, Alert, Alert! We're using special symbols here!—don't search for an *actual* question mark!" Then we select the subheading field and click Not (since we want all records that do *not* have any character in the subheading field):

find <u>not</u>:   ?

But of course there is a lot more we can do with the "any character" symbol; we can combine it with letters, numbers, and so on. So suppose we did a search for *?arry*. What would that probably give us? It might yield *harry, tarry*—any character followed by "arry." This is the shape I've been talking about. It is a very specific combination of letters, but the wildcard gives it the flexibility of finding *anything* that matches that general shape.

Now let's try creating a pattern. Suppose I want to find anything shaped like the following words: cat, cut, cot, yacht. Look at those words for a moment. What is the unique shape that describes them, that we could get your Martian to understand? In English, we can describe it as any word that has the letters c and then t with one letter between them. In Martian, we want to say "any character" instead, so: the letter c followed by any character followed by t. And finally, in symbols:

find: c?t   (or in CINDEX 3: c.t)

Of course, what the software finds is not limited to those four words, but anything that fits the shape. And you can see that the software will ignore everything else: in *yacht*, the y and a are irrelevant, as the pattern is just looking for c + any character + t (and what comes after or before that is ignored). Now, if I change the pattern a little bit, what would this do?:

find: ?c?t

In Martian, this is "any character followed by c, then any character, then t." Looking back at our four words (assuming they stand alone), which ones would this second pattern catch? Answer: only *yacht*, which has a character before the c. Now, another variation. Suppose I want to find anything in the shape of *cart, cent, clot, cast, raincoat,* or *chatting.* What is the unique shape here? Answer: two letters between the c and the t. So in Martian: *c* followed by any two characters followed by t:

> *find:*   c??t

Any Number of Characters

By itself, "any character" has limited possibilities. What if I don't know how many characters are between my two letters, or I want that to be flexible? Then I need the symbol for "any number of characters." Here there is more variation in the programs (consult the tables at the end of the chapter):

CINDEX 2:	?*
CINDEX 3:	.*
MACREX:	?*
SKY:	*

Note that this symbol means "any number of characters, *including none.*" So if we use the pattern c?*t (or c*t in SKY; c.*t in CINDEX 3), what words would it capture, or find? Take a minute to look at that before you read on. If the pattern, in Martian, is "c followed by any number of letters and then t," try making up a word list of what you would catch.

The pattern c?*t would pick up any of the following words, for example: *cart, cat chart, act, actor, yacht.* Note that *act* and *actor* have *no* characters between c and t, since this catches any number of characters, including none. (For "one or more characters" instead, consult the tables at the end of the chapter.)

Politics to Eco-Politics

Now let's look at another pattern question, based on the limited vocabulary we've covered so far. Suppose that you are partway through an index, and you get a message from the author to the effect that you need to change all of your political terms to eco-political, when they are at the beginning of a subheading or main heading. So *political, policies, politicians,* and *politics* need to be changed to *eco-political, eco-policies, eco-politicians,* and *eco-politics.* So how would we do this with a pattern?

Following our translation method, first we need to formulate the problem in English, then translate it to Martian, and then finally into the pattern symbols. The first part is always the "find" pattern. In order to make this change, we need to isolate the terms/records that we want to change. We don't want to add "eco-" to *every* word, just these few political terms. So, for our first attempt, suppose we say we want to find every instance of "pol" and change it to "eco-pol" when at the beginning of a field. If we tried this as a pattern, we might find that it caught some words we didn't want, such as *flagpoles* or *Poland.* So, for the second attempt, how would we exclude those? How about subheadings or main headings beginning with "poli" and followed by any letters after that? Yes, it looks like that will work.

So, translate this to Martian, and then to symbols. First, I need to introduce you to a new concept in Martian. Rather than "any heading that begins with ...," for our Martian high school helper we need to say "at the beginning of a field." This means at the beginning of the main heading, subheading, or locator field. (We know that there won't be any locator fields starting with this, so we can just ignore that, and let it match *any* field.) Then the full "find" pattern (we haven't even gotten to "change to" yet!) in Martian will be "find, at the beginning of the field, 'poli' followed by any number of characters."

In order to translate into software symbols, we need to introduce the symbols for "at the beginning of the field." In CINDEX and MACREX this is ^, and in SKY < (you can see in the tables at the end of the chapter that there are also symbols for "at the end of the field"). So, staying again with CINDEX 2, our pattern for "at the beginning of the field, 'poli' followed by any number of characters" will be:

find: ^poli?*

THE OTHER SHOE HITS THE FLOOR: REPLACE PATTERNS

Now, the second half of the task is to *change* it, so it's time to introduce replace patterns. These are much simpler than find patterns, with fewer symbols. But remember to always backup your index before running a replace pattern, in case it does not go as expected.

Before finishing the eco-poli problem just given, I want to demonstrate the simplest form of replace. Without using any symbols at all, we could replace *c* with *C*, for example, or replace *and* with *or*. This is not using patterns, but it shows how we can use regular letters in a "replace," in addition to the applicable pattern symbols.

Replacing With the "Same Thing"

Let's return to our fruit illustration. Remember that we can take a find pattern and add something to the end of it, in this case adding a banana:

find: apple
replace with: apple + banana

We've explored various ways of finding whatever we want with find patterns, but how do we communicate how to replace what we want? How do we say "apple plus banana"?

To pursue this, let's continue with the eco-poli problem. We need to replace *poli-whatever* with *eco-poliwhatever*. But when replacing, "whatever" is not good enough! If I catch the word *politician* with this pattern, I need to get back the same word—eco-politician or eco-politics, not eco-polifuzzblatt or something. So "whatever" is good enough for finding the words I want, allowing me that flexibility, but for replacing, I need to replace it with the *same* word, adding "eco-" to the front (that's the English).

So in Martian, we need to "find headings beginning with 'poli' followed by any number of characters (as we saw above) and replace it with 'eco-' followed by *the same characters we just matched*." What we need in the way of replace patterns is not "any character" nor "any number of characters" (any old characters will not do), but a symbol for "the whole thing just matched." Here they are:

CINDEX:	\&
MACREX default:	^&
SKY:	{0}

And we finally have the tools to complete the pattern:

find:	^poli?*
replace with:	eco-\&

To restate, this pattern finds any headings beginning with words starting "poli" ("poli" followed by any number of characters) and then replaces this with "eco-" followed by the whole thing we just matched.

Here's another simple replace using "the whole thing just matched": Suppose you have a group of entries for which you want to add "and" to any and all subheadings. Before you read on for the solution to this, try formulating this problem in English, in Martian, and then in the symbol language for your software.

In English, this is "add 'and' to the end of all subheadings." In Martian, as you recall, we need to use "find and replace" instead of "add," so we have "find any characters in the subheading field and replace with the same thing followed by a space and 'and'." And finally in symbols:

find:	?*	[selecting "subheading"]
replace with:	\& and	

Is this clear? If not, go back and review the part that is tripping you up before going on.

ADDITIONAL "FIND" TOOLS

When doing find patterns, we are not limited to "any character" or "any number of characters in combination with "real" letters and numbers; there are a lot of other possibilities that expand the vocabulary we can work with. Sometimes you want something more specific than "any character," and here are some of that ways to do that:

- Any letter

- Capital/lowercase letter

- Digit

- A choice of specific characters or digits

- Location in the field

Location in the Field

Earlier we saw "at the beginning," which is one of the location identifiers. The other most commonly used is "at the end," and this is symbolized by $ in CINDEX and MACREX and by > in SKY. So if we want to find any heading that ends with the word *Society*, then this is the pattern:

CINDEX/MACREX:	*find:*	Society$
SKY:	*find:*	Society>

You can see that this is really saying to find "the word *Society* followed by the end of the field." Similarly, if you wanted to find any records with headings ending with a close parentheses, the pattern would be)$ or)>.

Here's another example that uses the symbols for both beginning and end: find records that begin with the word *wolf* followed by any number of characters, with a parenthesis at the end." Take a minute to figure that out before reading on:

find: ^wolf?*)$

This may look like gobbledygook (the technical term for it), but you can parse it by taking each piece and decoding it, starting with ^.

Character Sets

The other options for being more specific than "any character" mostly use character sets (or "character lists"), which gives a set of characters that allows the software to match *any* character among those choices. CINDEX, MACREX, and SKY all use square brackets for these. So "[aeiou]" would be a character set meaning "any vowel." Here is an example pattern similar to what we used before; see if you can decode it:

find: c[aeiou]t

So what words would this pattern catch? How would it come out differently that the c?t we used before? It still matches one character, but now that character must be a vowel. So it can find *cat* but not *yacht* because the latter has a non-vowel between c and t.

There are also some pre-defined sets that you can use, such as [0–9] for any digit or [a–z] for any lowercase letter. Your software may have named sets or other symbols as well; consult the tables at the end of the chapter or your software user guide for those.

Putting together the character sets with the location symbols, suppose you want to find all records with subheadings that begin with a year in the 1900s or 2000s. Again you are figuring out what is unique about what you want to find, and in this case the subheading must start with a four-digit number. And further, the first digit must be 1 or 2 and the second digit must be 0 or 9. So:

find: ^[12][09][0-9][0-9]

You can see how the *options* that character sets represent can give you endless possibilities for what you want to find. Once you are comfortable with "any character" and "any number of characters," you can explore working with character sets; I will not be emphasizing the latter in this chapter.

WORKING WITH "CHUNKS"

Previously we worked with "the whole thing we just matched," but patterns also let you get fancier than that. Sometimes you will need to identify specific parts of what you are matching, rather than simply the entire thing. Remember from the earlier fruit illustration that one thing we could do was rearrange them:

find: apple + banana + pear
replace with: pear + banana + apple

This is a powerful tool with patterns, and it allows you to do a lot that "whatever we just matched" would not. An example that follows this fruit pattern would be to replace headings like *cats and dogs* or *fire engines and police cars* to *dogs and cats* or *police cars and fire engines*. I call this working with "chunks"—we have chunk #1 followed by "and" followed by chunk #2, and we are swapping the chunks. These "chunks" are sometimes called subpatterns (in CINDEX) or pattern groups (in SKY).

So you can see here that rather than getting the software to identify "the whole thing just matched," we need to be able to identify these chunks individually and that allows us to move them around, or even leave some of them out, as we want. Another example of applying the chunks would be if you want to change something like *American Society for Indexing (ASI)* to *ASI (American Society for Indexing)*—and yes, I know that some programs have a "flip" function to do this with a click, but patterns allow you to do them all at once. This pattern is the one I use more than any other.

To apply the English/Martian/Symbols method to formulating this first problem (*cats and dogs*) take a moment to figure out how you would say this in English and then translate to Martian and then symbols. (We are assuming that you have already isolated into a group the records you want to change—you can do this by using finds and/or find patterns.)

English: We have text before and after "and" in a heading, and we want to switch them. Another way of saying this, that gets us partway toward the Martian language: Find text that looks like this—"a first chunk of text followed by 'and' followed by a second chunk of text"—and replace it with this—"chunk one followed by 'and' followed by chunk two." This sounds kind of complicated, I know, but this may help:

find:	chunk #1 and chunk #2
replace with:	chunk #2 and chunk #1

Our Martian helper, as might be expected, doesn't know the word *text*, but we've already learned how to get around that, by saying "any number of characters" instead. That gets us close to what we need for the symbol language of the software. For CINDEX 2 and SKY, we indicate these chunks by putting them in braces { } and CINDEX 3 uses parentheses instead. (My understanding is that MACREX uses a function other than patterns to make this type of change.) And inside we just need to put those symbols we already learned for "any number of characters":

CINDEX 2:	*find:*	{?*} and {?*}
CINDEX 3	*find:*	(.*) and (.*)
SKY:	*find:*	{*} and {*}

The chunks are numbered in order, so the first one is chunk #1, without needing to be labeled as such. So this find pattern reads as "find one chunk of any number of characters, followed by 'and,' followed by a second chunk of any number of characters." Now all we need to do is tell the software to put chunk #2 first and chunk #1 last. In Martian this is: "replace with the first chunk, followed by 'and,' followed by the second chunk." And here it is:

CINDEX: *replace with:*   \2 and \1
SKY: *replace with:*   {2} and {1}

You can see that the replace patterns are fairly simple, once you know how to read them. You can use any combination of real characters (such as "and") along with the symbol for "the whole thing just matched" or the symbols for specific chunks matched.

Expert Tip

A note on the use of the backslash in CINDEX: The backslash is used three different ways in CINDEX. In a replace pattern, it points to a chunk: \2 is "chunk #2, or \& refers to "the whole thing just matched." In a find pattern, however, the backslash turns a special character into a regular character. If you want to find a $, for example, you have to let CINDEX know that is what you really want, instead of treating it as a special symbol meaning "end of field." So in a find pattern, \$ will search for an actual $ character. And finally, the third use of the backslash in CINDEX is to introduce a special operation. See your software manual for more on this.

The Acronym Flip

Let's try another example: switching text inside and outside parentheses, such as acronyms. You may want to use this to double post entries like *American Society for Indexing (ASI)* and *bakeries (patisseries)* to *ASI (American Society for Indexing)* and *patisseries (bakeries)*. (You can see that this doesn't have to be an acronym; this pattern works for any alternate terms in parentheses you want to flip.)

First, you have conducted finds to isolate only the records you want to change into a group, so that other records in the index will not be affected, (and of course, you have backed up your index before running the pattern in case something goes unexpectedly).

In English: Find text followed by text in parentheses, and switch them. In Martian: find a chunk of any number of characters at the beginning of a field followed by a second chunk of any number of characters inside parentheses. Replace this with chunk #2 followed by chunk #1 in parentheses. Symbol language (using the CINDEX 2 pattern):

find: ^{?*} ({?*})

replace with: \2 (\1)

Do you see how this pattern works? Can you look at the pattern and decode what it means? Refer to the tables at the end of the chapter if you are having trouble reading it.

One thing I want to point out about this pattern: See how the parentheses are *outside* the braces? The pattern would not work otherwise, because we want to move the text *inside* the parentheses, but leave the parentheses where they are. We don't want to drag the parentheses along with chunk #2 and have them fall at the beginning of the heading. What would happen if we did it the other way instead?

find: ^{?*} {(?*)}

replace with: \2 (\1)

This would take:

bakeries (patisseries)

and change it to:

(patisseries) (bakeries)

Not what you wanted! Can you see why it does this? The original parentheses around *patisseries* are included as part of chunk #2, since they are inside the braces, and so they get moved along with the word *patisseries* to the beginning as part of the chunk. And then the new parentheses in the replace pattern are still added around chunk #1, now at the end. You can fix such a mistake with another pattern!

Expert Tip

I use this acronym flip pattern so much that I am in the habit of adding "acro" in hidden text to any records I'm going to want to use it on. So then all I need in order to isolate the group of records is do a "find all" for "acro."

Some Additional Pattern Examples

Good news: We have covered all the basic concepts of patterns: wildcard symbols for "any character," "any number of characters," character sets, chunks, and replace patterns. I will conclude with a few more examples. The possibilities are endless, which is why I've focused on the *process* of turning a problem into a pattern; if you understand the logic and the language, then you can formulate patterns for many problems that may arise while indexing, rather than needing to rely on patterns given to you.

Move "And" to the End

Here, finally, we're getting back to the problem where you have a lot of subheadings beginning with "and," and you want to move all those "ands" to the end. Whenever you want to "move" something, that is an indication that you will be using chunks.

In Martian: Find all subheadings with "and" at the beginning of the field, followed by a space and a chunk of any number of characters to the end of the field. Replace this with the chunk followed by a space, followed by "and." (Note the importance of the space—we don't want to tack on "and" to the end of the last word, without a space.)

find:	^and {?*}$
replace with:	\1 and

Women's Names

Here is one Sherry Smith sent me. She had an index with a lot of names of married women with their unmarried surnames in parentheses, as follows:

Gee, Sandra (born Eff)

and these needed to be double posted as:

Eff, Sandra (later Gee)

This is another case of moving things around, but in this instance we have more pieces. Since this is double-posting, don't forget to duplicate all the entries once they are found in a group. We need to run the "find" pattern first, creating a temporary group, and then duplicate that group to have records that we now want to change. (I almost always follow this method of running the find pattern first, so I can see exactly what records will be changed before running the replace pattern.)

Then we need to rearrange each piece (Gee, Sandra, and Eff) and insert punctuation, parentheses, and "later" where appropriate, while leaving "born" out of the replaced entries. We could make "born" one of the chunks, but since it is always the same word, "born," and we don't need to keep it, then we can just type the word in the find pattern without making it a chunk.

We can divide out the various pieces of the original entry, using both chunks and regular characters:

Gee + comma + Sandra + (+ born + Eff +)

and if Gee is chunk #1, Sandra is chunk #2, and Eff is chunk #3, then our pattern is:

find:	^{?*}, {?*} (born {?*})
replace with:	\3, \2 (later \1)

(If you didn't quite follow that, then use the English, Martian, symbols process to get yourself there.)

Spacing With Initials in Names

I sometimes get texts that are inconsistent in the spacing of names with initials: J.A. Smith and P. T. Barnum. After entering them as they are in the text, I may eventually notice the inconsistency, query the client, and then need to adjust my entries. Assuming the client wants the space added in, what would the pattern be to change all the names with no space between the initials?

The first step is always to figure out how to find the records you want. What is unique about them? Here we could search for a capital letter followed by a period followed by a capital letter followed by another period, but we can do it more simply than that. Most likely, there are no other cases of a period followed by a capital letter. So we can just try doing that find, and see if that gives us any records that fall outside of the initials issues. For a capital letter, character sets come into play. There is more than one way to do it, but this works as well as any:

find:	.{[A-Z]}
replace with:	. \1

(As explained earlier, a special character such as the period in CINDEX 3 would require a backslash before it in order to turn it into a literal period: "\.".)

This pattern illustrates how we can actually match just a very small portion of the heading, if that is all that is needed to recognize what we're finding and then change it.

A Cookbook Question From the CINDEXusers List

Ina Gravitz posted the following question to the CINDEXusers List:

> I'm indexing a cookbook in which some dishes are ingredients of other dishes. The recipes for these dishes are given as recipes, so I have:
>
> > Longaniza, 183 (this is the recipe itself)
> > Longaniza
> >   as ingredient, 47
>
> I'd like a pattern for raising the sub-one-level *as ingredient* to the main heading and having a comma. So the first entry would be *Longaniza, as ingredient*. Without manually changing each entry is that possible?

And here is Connie Binder's answer on the list (edited a bit):

> Make a copy of your index so if this doesn't work, you haven't lost anything.
>
> First, *find all* for *as ingredient* in Sub1 field. That will make a separate group so you can just deal with those.
>
> Second, add *as ingredient* to the main heading using a pattern:
>
> | | | |
> |---|---|---|
> | *Find*: | ^?*$ | [Field: Main; "pattern" box checked] |
> | *Change to*: | \&, as ingredient | |
>
> Third, delete the *as ingredient* subheading:
>
> | | | |
> |---|---|---|
> | *Find*: | as ingredient | [Field: Sub 1; Pattern box unchecked] |
> | *Change to*: | (leave blank) | |

This is a great example of a multi-step pattern, and the question is something you might initially think cannot be done with patterns at all, because patterns will not allow you to move a word or phrase from one field to another. But in this case, the phrase is the same every time (*as ingredient*), so once Ina had isolated the records she wanted to change into a temporary group, then every main heading needed the same phrase, preceded by a comma, added to the end. And a second replace serves to delete the phrase from the subheading (leaving the "change to" box blank ends up deleting the matched text by replacing it with nothing). So keep in mind that you sometimes will need multiple steps, and sometimes using multiple steps might simply be easier. Another application of multiple steps is to run several "find" patterns, each time narrowing down your temporary group until you have exactly the records you want to run a replace pattern on.

Error Checking With "Find" Patterns

The examples just given all use find and replace, but there can be a lot of power in find pattern alone without replacing. Checking for common errors can be a useful way to use "find," with or without patterns, or using a combination of the two. Here are three examples of ways to use find pattern to check for errors.

First, suppose you are using an italicized *t* in locators for tables (182*t*), but you want to check whether you forgot to italicize any of those t's. This is a case when using multiple steps to narrow down your group will be helpful. First, you can use a pattern to locate all records that point to a table (all records that have a digit followed by a t in the page field):

Find: [0-9]t   [Field: Page]

Why didn't we just search for t in the page field? Because this would pick up a lot of cross-references that included a "t." Once you have isolated all these records with tables, then you only need to see the ones that *do not* have an italicized t:

Find: t   [Field: Page; Italics selected; NOT checked]

If there are any search results, then this will be your unitalicized t locators, and then you can simply replace t in the page field with t + italics on.

A second example of error checking might be years. If I'm doing a Renaissance-era text, I frequently find myself typing something like 1675 as 1975. But if you simply search for 19 you might come up with too much other stuff. So this one-step pattern will find all years beginning with 19:

Find: 19[0-9][0-9]

Then if there are a lot of them, you can do a simple find/replace to change 19 to 16.

The third error-checking example (thanks to Enid Zafran) involves an index of legal cases with full citations. One error check is a multi-step search for any records without "v." in them. First is a simple search for *NOT* "v." in the main heading field. A lot of what results will be "in re" and "ex parte" cases, which do not need a "v.", so the next step is to search for *NOT* in re and *NOT* ex parte. Then what is left can be checked for errors: There might be instances of V. (should be lower case), or v without the period, or cases with the v left out entirely. This series of narrowing searches serves to pinpoint such possible errors (or find that there are none!). And since every case with citation should end with a close parenthesis, an additional search, this one using a pattern, can reveal if there are any stray entries that are missing that legal citation by checking for any records that do not have a parenthesis at the end of the main heading:

Find:)$ [Field: Main; NOT checked]

So there are many types of errors that you can check for using single or multiple searches with patterns or without.

These few examples provide only a taste of what can be done with patterns. Don't be afraid to explore your own solutions to indexing problems that can avoid, in Ina's words, "manually changing each entry." And when a pattern just isn't doing what you want (yes, it happens), take it to the users group for your software—there's a lot of great help out there.

Table 12.1   CINDEX Pattern Symbols

SYMBOLS in FIND Patterns		
CINDEX 2	**CINDEX 3**	**Meaning**
?	. *period*	any character (wildcard)
*	*	any number of occurrences, including none
	+	one or more occurrences of preceding element
?*	.*	any number of characters, including none
??*	.+	one or more characters
^	^	at beginning of field (first character)
$	$	at end of field (last character)
\	\	turns symbol into literal character (and other uses)
	.? *or* +?	matches *minimum* occurrence
	\b	at beginning of word ("word boundary")
	|	"or" (*dog*|*cat* will match *dog* or *cat*)
	{2} *or* {5} *etc*	exact number of repetitions: 2, 5, etc.
	?	zero or one occurrence of preceding element
{}	( )	subpattern/pattern groups ("chunks")

SYMBOLS in REPLACE Patterns		
CINDEX 2	CINDEX 3	Meaning
\&	\&	the *whole* thing you just matched
\1 etc.	\1 etc.	refers to first subpattern (or 2nd, etc.)
+	+	change to uppercase (whatever it follows)
-	-	change to lowercase (whatever it follows)
CHARACTER SETS		
CINDEX 2	CINDEX 3	Meaning
[ ]	[ ]	indicates a set or character list
- hyphen	- hyphen	in character list, for range, such as [A-Z]
^	^	at begin of character list, means *not*
[a-z]	[a-z]	any lowercase letter
[A-Z]	[A-Z]	any uppercase letter
[a-zA-z]	[a-zA-z]	any letter of the alphabet
[0-9]	[0-9]	any digit
	[: :]	predefined set
	[:letter:]	any letter

Table 12.2   MACREX Pattern Symbols

SYMBOLS in MATCHING patterns	
Symbol	Function
?	any character
*	any number of occurrences, including none
+	one or more occurrences of preceding element
^	at beginning of line (first character)
$	at end of line (last character)
:a	any alphabetic character
:d	any digit (numeric) character
:n	any alphanumeric character
:m	spaces and other non-alphanumeric characters
\	turns symbol into literal character
CHARACTER SETS	
Symbol	Function
[ ]	indicates character list or set
^	at begin of character list, means *not*

Table 12.3   SKY Pattern Symbols

SYMBOLS in FIND patterns	
Symbol	Function
?	any single character
*	any number of characters, including none
?*	one or more characters
<	at beginning of field (first character)
>	at end of field (last character)
[ ]	turn a symbol into a literal character, e.g. [?] [*]
#	any single digit 0-9
&	whole number
~	word
{ }	pattern groups (subpatterns or "chunks")
SYMBOLS in REPLACE patterns	
Symbol	Function
{0}	the *whole* thing you just matched
{1} *or* {2} etc.	in replace pattern, refers to first/second pattern group, etc.
CHARACTER LISTS	
Symbol	Function
[ ]	indicates character list or set
- *hyphen*	in character list, for range, such as [A-Z]
!	at begin of character list, means *not*
[a-z]	any lowercase letter
[A-Z]	any uppercase letter
[a-zA-z]	any letter of the alphabet (be sure to check the Match Case box)

Chapter 13

Teaching Indexing

Lucie Haskins © 2014

I love talking about indexing, especially to people whose eyes don't glaze over when they listen. So, when the opportunity came along a few years ago to teach for the online University of California–Berkeley (UCB) indexing course, I couldn't believe my good fortune. Here was a ready-made audience eager to dialogue with *me* about indexing and all things indexing-related! A match made in heaven.

As a teacher, I take great pleasure in figuring out how to explain a complex concept in a simple, clear, and logical way. (It's really true that, if you want to learn more about a subject, just teach it.) I love the excitement that my students radiate as they work through the lessons and immerse themselves in the world of indexing. They energize me and invigorate me.

I believe that my job as a teacher is two-fold: First, to help my students learn about indexing to the best of their abilities, and second, to help them grow and stretch in their practical application of that knowledge. If I do my job well, by the time my students finish the course, they'll know *if* indexing is what they really want to pursue and, if so, they'll have a solid foundation on which to build their businesses.

And with each student I reach, I feel like I'm paying it forward in gratitude to all those established indexers who helped *me* just 15 short years ago when *I* was that fledgling indexing student and that newbie freelance indexer.

INTERACTIONS WITH ONLINE STUDENTS

Online learning can be a very remote experience (both for the students and the teacher) because of the limitations in communicating without face-to-face interactions. However, I've found that the communication channels we've set up for our UCB indexing students go a long way toward surmounting these difficulties. As a testament to the effectiveness of these channels, I've developed very real and very personal relationships with a lot of my former students. (Whenever I have the opportunity to meet some of my students face to face, it's always been a true joy and absolute delight.)

I interact with my students in the following ways:

- *Weekly chats:* We hold these during the official "office hour" in a chat room that instructors take turns facilitating. Students are invited to bring any and all indexing-related questions, and the conversation can get quite lively.

- *Responding to student postings:* Students post responses to end-of-unit questions as well as informally in the "student forum." Other students join in and pretty soon, there's an interesting exchange going on. I read each posting and interact by clarifying unclear concepts or by spurring on additional discussion.

- *Feedback for student assignments:* I personalize my feedback for each student and each unit assignment. My feedback includes observations, suggestions, and clarifications about indexing concepts that might have been misapplied or otherwise need to be improved on. Sometimes I also send along interesting indexing-related articles, sample indexes, and anything else that might be considered helpful.

- *My personal reflections at the completion of each unit:* I include a personal reflection with my feedback for each student assignment. These reflections are pre-crafted to apply to some aspect of that unit's topic. The reflections might discuss my early days as an indexer, the details involved in setting up my business, how I enjoy embedded indexing, my step-by-step indexing process and final edit checklist, or just my thoughts about the next steps my students might want to take. (I've included my final reflection to my indexing students at the end of this article.)

PROGRESSING THROUGH THE MODULES

The UCB indexing course provides a six-month window from signup to course completion. As with anything else in life, how successfully students complete the course depends on their motivation and adherence to the recommended timeframes.

To help students remain on track, they receive a time management spreadsheet template that identifies the maximum amount of time they should allow for each module. They enter their course start date into the template and the spreadsheet calculates the maximum time they should spend on each module—automatically factoring in more time for more complex modules.

Each module introduces specific indexing concepts for students to absorb. When they feel ready, they then complete the end-of-module assignments (one at a time) to demonstrate their understanding of the concepts just studied. Depending on module topics, assignments range from extremely simple to more thought- and effort-provoking.

REVIEWING STUDENT ASSIGNMENTS

Online courses provide a safe learning environment to allow students to hone their indexing skills, where one mistake won't lose them a client, as might happen in the "real" world. My feedback is geared to provide as much information as possible, in an encouraging and helpful manner, while providing that safety net to shore them up as they learn. Grades are important. Feedback is important. In an online environment especially, students exist in a vacuum until they receive them. So it's imperative to provide timely feedback for student assignments—to correct misapplied concepts, to recognize and celebrate their successes, and to foster that burgeoning relationship with them.

I return simpler assignments (graded via answer sheets) within one to two days. More complex assignments (such as indexes), I return within one week. I typically spend a few hours reviewing student indexes line-by-line while searching for (1) patterns in indexing, (2) examples of misapplied concepts, (3) examples where they've nailed the concepts, and (4) examples where they've demonstrated they see the big picture while also focusing on the details. I comment on relevant index entries and also summarize my impressions.

BACKGROUND AND MOTIVATION OF MY STUDENTS

The students in my section are a diverse bunch, with widely varied backgrounds and skill sets, including: computer programmers, librarians, stay-at-home moms, editors, book sellers/buyers, technical writers, weather forecasters, accountants, marine biologists, and educators. Most are tired of their current situation (whether it's the corporate rat race or just looking for something "more"). They are all ready for a lifestyle change and want to *do* something meaningful and make a difference with their lives. Some are ready to take on a new full-time career; others are about to retire but still want to work part-time to supplement their retirement income; still others have dropped out to raise a family and need to add to the family coffers but also want to stay at home and care for the kids while doing so. (The possibility of working from home is a huge draw for many students.)

These students invariably have a thirst for knowledge and are widely read, highly educated, and highly motivated. They are committed to learning, and they accept responsibility for steering their destiny and taking action toward fulfilling their dreams, whatever those dreams might be. What more could a teacher ask for?

WHO IS A SUCCESSFUL STUDENT ANYWAY?

Students who thrive on shaping and organizing information are definitely in the right place. They excel in their indexing studies, pick up the concepts quickly, and apply them beautifully on their practice indexes.

But I've seen other students struggle to find their footing—sometimes finding it after a reassessment and recommitment to the effort involved, other times not. Students who withdraw from the course do so for a variety of reasons:

- *They took on too much of a commitment without realizing the level of effort that would be required.* They didn't realize just how much work would be needed to learn about indexing concepts and then apply that knowledge in the practical exercises.

- *They realized that indexing wasn't the right career choice for them after all.* Perhaps they read the *Money* magazine article from years ago that listed indexing as an easy way to make money at home just by reading books. As students work through the first assignments, they might be surprised to find they have difficulty following instructions or understanding the indexing concepts (no matter how many times they reread the material). They might completely misinterpret what the assignments require and produce something that they have to completely redo, or they get stuck and can't progress through the modules at a steady pace. As time progresses and circumstances don't improve, this is when they re-evaluate and realize that "Thanks, but no thanks, this isn't for me."

- *They realized they really weren't comfortable working as freelancers without a perceived safety net.* The idea of not having a regular paycheck *and* having to drum up their own business just didn't sit well with them.

- *Life had other plans.* Students cleared their calendars and started the course and really enjoyed it. And then their spouse lost his job. Or their parents got really ill and need extended care. Or … Or … Or. I fit into this category about 15 years ago. I had started the USDA indexing course (the only one available at that time and now called the Graduate School USA) with the greatest of intentions. And then life interrupted. I couldn't complete the course because I needed to help my parents with long-term and severe medical problems. I applied for an extension and thought I'd get back on track "soon." Then life interrupted again and I got *another* extension! I finally finished but it took me *three years* to complete that *one-year* course. (Many thanks to my instructor Jan

Wright for never giving up on me!) I *knew* indexing was absolutely the right career choice for me but, at that time in my life, in the midst of crazy circumstances out of my control, even that knowledge and that certainty weren't enough to allow me to complete my studies when life got in the way of my oh-so-carefully-crafted plans.

- *Students didn't care for the online delivery mechanism after they've tried it out.* They found they really needed the face-to-face contact after all and didn't do well without it.

I *also* count these withdrawals as successes. These students might not have selected indexing as a career choice, but well-thought-out decisions *not* to move forward with indexing clear the road for other (perhaps better suited) pursuits, hopefully with more clarity of purpose than before. And that is a very valuable awareness to have.

DROPOUT RATES I SEE

Online classes typically have very high attrition rates, often as much as 30 to 40 percent or even more. We attribute this most often to students being adults with lives that get in the way (as I've described), rather than dissatisfaction with the classes themselves.

The UCB indexing classes, in general, seem to have a higher completion rate than most online courses. Some years have shown completion rates for UCB indexing students in the 70th percentile; other years, higher completion rates have been recorded—which is exceptional. (For an interesting and thorough discussion about completion rates for the major online indexing courses, read Enid L. Zafran's "The Newbies" article in the March 2013 issue of *Key Words*.)

WHAT SEEMS LIKE THE HARDEST PART FOR STUDENTS

In life, everyone has to acquire knowledge and master skills in a new profession or field of study. They aren't born with that knowledge or those skills. Students in this course are no different. But students don't just learn about indexing during their six months. They also have to master two other areas at the same time: learning new software applications (and computers if not already tech-savvy), and the discipline of self-study. All three prongs need to be successfully managed in a compressed time period (6 months).

New learning curves can be difficult to face at any age but are especially so for adult learners who haven't been in a formal study program for many years, if not decades. These students can quickly become overwhelmed and discouraged as they start from scratch and climb one painful rung at a time to regain those study habits and achieve elusive subject matter mastery.

I've found that the best background for indexing students is an eclectic one, with a little knowledge of this and a little knowledge of that. Because the more areas students have been exposed to (and tried and succeeded in), the more successes they've already experienced in mastering new skills and the more confidence they can bring with them as they tackle another learning curve. If students can remember those past successes and also remember that (1) everyone encounters challenges in their lifetime and (2) that the way to deal with each challenge is to just work through it—one step at a time, one exercise at a time—they can stay on track and persevere and finish the course.

In a way, the indexing class is a microcosm of the real world. There are always problems, challenges, and interruptions to face in life. How students deal with these during the course and how adaptable they are in resolving them can determine how successful they become in their indexing businesses.

HOW PEOPLE REACT TO HAVING TO MASTER THREE SOFTWARE APPLICATIONS

Even though they grumble, most students eventually appreciate being able to "test drive" each of the "big three" indexing programs (CINDEX, MACREX, and SKY) during the course. While it's a steep learning curve, they grin and bear it for the first few units that require using all three programs. In effect, they are demo-ing each of the software packages, in a controlled environment, with technical support available from all three vendors as well as from their instructors. And what better place is there to learn something new than in a safe and supportive environment?

The course's intent is to get the students familiar with each of these programs so that by the time the students work on their first "real" indexing assignment (about midway through the course), they have had enough practice with all the programs to *know* which one they like the best. From that point on, they select the software package they want to use for each assignment.

That experience wasn't available when I learned indexing back in the mid-1990s. So when the time came for me to purchase my indexing software, I didn't know which program was the right one for me. I had to quickly research all three, work through the demos on my own, make my selection, and cross my fingers that I had made the right decision.

I think the UCB indexing course approach to software is effective, important, and a helpful component. It's certainly a lot kinder than the trial-by-fire decision-making process I went through as a trying-to-get-established indexer.

WHAT STUDENTS SEEM TO LIKE

My students' feedback invariably lists the following components as important elements of their studies:

- *Learning all aspects of indexing (both the theoretical information and the informal reflections and communication)*: That's why the students enroll. They want to learn a new craft/skill.

- *Interactions with other students and their instructor* (through student forums, chat sessions, emails, and phone calls)

- *Personalized and thorough feedback on their unit assignments*: I still remember how eagerly I awaited Jan's feedback on my assignments in the USDA course—how helpful it was and how I devoured and studied that feedback afterward. In turn, I strive to provide that same experience to my students, by including as much detailed and helpful information as possible. (Nothing beats getting a line-by-line review of your index—that also points out patterns that need to be addressed and concepts that need more review—all the while pointing out areas that were beautifully executed.)

CONCLUSION

Freelancing as an indexer can be difficult and may not be for everyone. But for me, after 12 years, I can't imagine going back to a 9-to-5 job. I'm spoiled for life. I create my successes, and I'm not dependent on being in the good graces of my boss in order to progress as I'd like to. It's all up to me to please my clients and manage my business affairs.

Anything I can do to promote this profession and help train the next generation of indexers is both my honor and my privilege. Remember that aphorism "A rising tide lifts all boats?" So, so true. I see our indexing community as appendages of one body and our combined strength coming from our individual but interconnected members. Encouraging fledgling and wannabe indexers to succeed and thrive only helps us all. I'd like to close by sharing with all of you my final reflection letter to my indexing students.

FINAL REFLECTION LETTER TO YOU

Well here it is, my final reflection letter to you. I have to confess that this letter was extremely difficult to compose, and I'm not really sure if its contents are what you expect but they were what I felt drawn to writing. I feel an overwhelming responsibility in what advice I'm going to share with you … and I've been going back and forth and back and forth in what to include. If I included everything, it would be a book! (ah! now *that's* a great idea … perhaps I should create a book-let—sometime down the road—of assembled words of wisdom for you fledgling indexers!) In the meantime, I need to distill my thoughts and provide you with marching orders as you start your frightening, but oh-so-wonderful, journey into the world of freelance indexing.

Dream Big and Hold On to Your Dreams

First and foremost, I advise you to hold on to your dreams … and to dream big! You have done what 50 percent or more of those "interested" in indexing haven't done: enrolled *and completed* a basic indexing course. Kudos to you! You deserve it! Now, while the satisfaction and thrill of having completed this course is still fresh, it is the perfect time to sit down and think about the future and how you want to shape your indexing career.

Identify Your Indexing Niche and Timeframe for Meeting Your Goals

What are your goals? Do you want to index full-time? Immediately? Within a certain timeframe? What does indexing full-time mean to you? Do you have a certain income you'd like to earn per month? A certain number of hours you'd like to work every day? What areas would you like to specialize in? What did you study in school? What are your hobbies? Interests? What job skills do you have? Those are all potential specialty areas. What publishers are there in your fields of interest? Have you checked to see if your local library has *Literary Market Place*? This is an absolutely wonderful reference (two volumes) that identifies publishers by industry and provides lots of valuable information about how many books they publish each year (you probably want to market to a company that publishes at least 50 books per year … after all you want to get repeat business … in your lifetime!).

Create Your Business Plan and Set Up Your Business

What do you need to do to reach your goals? Do you have an office space? What do you need to purchase for your office? Have you seen my short 2-minute video that does a 360-degree sweep of my office (www.youtube.com/watch?v=or-79hpCCec)? Do you have all your needed equipment? Think about the computer and applications you'll need. Think about ergonomics: desk, chair, monitors, and so on. What about reference books? Printer, internet access, fax capability (I still like having a fax though many indexers don't have this capability), office supplies (reams of paper, post-it notes, and so on), a copy machine (part of the printer?), and scanner (again, part of the printer?). Do you have a backup plan? What will you do if the electricity goes off or if your computer dies? What about membership in the

American Society for Indexing (ASI)? Printing business cards? How will you generate invoices? Track your expenses and income? Set up a separate savings/checking account for your business? Checking if you need to comply with local/state regulations regarding business licensing/registration? What about your indexing knowledge? What do you have deficiencies in? How will you resolve them? By when? What knowledge is still tenuous? Missing? How will you get it? By when? These are just a few items about what's involved in getting started and it's not meant to be a complete list. I strongly, strongly recommend that you check out the ever-increasing indexing-related articles, websites, and blogging sites available through the magic of the internet.

Market Yourself and Market Yourself and Market Yourself

Right off the bat, truly and deeply understand that you provide a much appreciated and needed service and that editors who deal with freelancers will be happy (maybe even *ecstatic*) to hear from someone able to help them with their constant dilemma of finding a reliable and competent indexer. (And you *are* competent! I'm a tough grader and you did very well in the class!)

How will you distinguish yourself from the other candidates? Make sure you treat yourself as a professional from day one. Do *not* quote ridiculously low starting rates to your client as it's almost impossible to get an existing client to raise the rates they've established with you. (In my 10-plus years of indexing, I have *never* had a client who agreed to rate increases.) Also, follow your gut instinct and take care in accepting new-to-you clients. Do some research (ask on the discussion lists) if you've been approached by clients you are not familiar with. Unfortunately, horror stories exist about how unwary indexers have been bamboozled by unethical clients out there.

If your clients pass initial muster, but you later find them cheap or difficult to work with, put them high on your "too busy with other projects" list and rid yourself of them after you've built up a decent clientele. (I currently have about 20 active clients—some clients are more active than others.) My clients have come and gone (for various reasons). That's the name of the game. Some of my best clients I've had for 10 years (as long as I've been indexing).

What will you do every day to market yourself until you get at least five clients? Every week? Every month? It's critical to get multiple clients so your business does not depend on the health of an individual client. Think outside the box for marketing:

- In the beginning, I culled information about potential indexing jobs that are sometimes posted on the discussion lists. I wasn't ready (at that time) to apply for those projects at the time the jobs were announced, but I thought that if editors have posted once about a job, they might need candidates later down the road, so

they would be a prescreened potential source for me when I was
ready to market. That's how I got my second client.

- Have one-on-one chats with other indexers at meetings. Don't talk
  to other indexers with the objective of marketing to them. Instead,
  talk to them with the idea of finding out what makes them tick and
  what their interests are. If you strike some common ground, they
  will remember you ... and potentially steer some indexing work
  your way. I got a *lot* of my clients during my second and third
  years of indexing in just this way.

- Talk to absolutely everyone about your exciting new career. Word
  of mouth is tremendously important and tremendously powerful in
  our small world. Expect that many people will obviously *not* be
  interested, but you'll be surprised at just how many people are
  fascinated to learn that real-live people index books! That's how I
  got my first indexing job.

- Research in *Literary Market Place* (as I already mentioned). Email
  editors (typically the production or managing editor). Or call if
  you are brave enough. Indexers have written and posted scripts for
  these kinds of phone calls. Research this possibility. Personally, I
  would rather starve than make a cold call but more power to you if
  you have no problems picking up that phone.

- Do *not* send unsolicited attachments (snail mail instead) and do *not*
  make them email you back to ask for more information. The best
  scenario is to have a simple website you can include in your blurb
  to the editor (do *not* send to a generic email ... find a real person's
  name!). That is the best of all worlds. If editors are interested, they
  will click the link to learn about your background, etc.

Be determined! Be proactive! It's *your* business and no one else is responsible
for doing all this for you. Remember, it typically takes about one to two years to
have a full-time client list. So what do you do in the meantime? If you need additional income, what other services can you provide? Web design? Editing?
Copywriting?

Expect Setbacks

You are going to encounter the typical (and frustrating) difficulties that each new
entrepreneur faces; they are just part of the startup process:

- The business aspects of setting up a business (e.g., quarterly taxes,
  recordkeeping, initial office purchases, business plan)

- Marketing and advertising your services

- Continuing education (e.g., via peer reviews, chapter meetings, regional/national conferences)

- Branding yourself and achieving name recognition (e.g., meetings, discussion lists, article writing)

And there are far better sources than myself that have already provided this information. Ferret them out. Check the discussion list archives for questions others have already asked about these topics. Find the more generalized books at the library or the more indexing-specific books at the Information Today, Inc. website, which publishes on behalf of ASI, including this book (books.infotoday. com/books/index.shtml#index). The ASI website (www.asindexing.org) is a great starting point for a lot of this information.

Remember: Your Reputation Is Everything

From day one, protect your reputation. How do you want to be known? As a professional? Is your word your bond? Are you always turning in good, accurate indexes on time? Are you minimal maintenance, or are you needy? That is, do editors need to hold your hand during indexing projects? Do you interrupt the editor's already busy day without thought to his workload? Are you aware of how overworked editors typically are? Do you follow guidelines and instructions to the letter? Are you easy to deal with? Are you fun to deal with? Picture that image of yourself in your mind and work hard every day to make sure that image shines!

You'll encounter situations where you'll need to negotiate things: deadlines, fee structure, what to include in the index, and so on. I've learned that one can approach negotiations in two different ways—for long-term relationships and for short-term relationships. It's important to know which type of client you're dealing with and which type of relationship you are looking to establish. If you don't care if you ever communicate with this client again, then you look out for yourself and stick to your guns regarding what you think is right. You'll probably lose the relationship because you are just looking out for yourself (win–lose) but that's okay in certain circumstances. If you are looking for a long-term (win–win) relationship with a client, then you have to tread more softly and investigate all aspects of a situation. What decisions and accommodations can you make that are beneficial to both sides in this negotiation?

Be cognizant that when established indexers refer work to you, they are placing their reputations on the line with the recommendations that they make. Do everything in your power to ensure that you live up to their expectations. When the opportunity comes for you to refer extra work to other indexers, pick carefully as their work will also reflect on you.

Pursue Continuing Education

I've been indexing over 10 years now and I'm still learning new things every year! What a vibrant and exciting niche this is! I just love it … and I love being able to continually expand my indexing skills and knowledge. Take advantage of all the opportunities to learn (both formally and informally) through all the mechanisms out there—peer reviews, discussion lists, reading articles and books on indexing topics, conferences, workshops, one-on-one meetings, chat sessions. Check out the new business module for the ASI training course (The Business of Indexing; www.asindexing.org/online-store/business-of-indexing-module) developed by Kate Mertes and Enid L. Zafran.

Give Back to the Indexing Community

Indexers are extremely generous. They give freely of their time and knowledge. Sharing freely is what makes this community so great, and you are now in a position to share. You've completed the course, therefore you know more than students who haven't completed the course. Find ways to give back to this community, whether by answering newbie indexer questions on the discussion lists or by volunteering at chapter meetings or even, eventually, at the national level.

An Offer for My Graduated Students

I am available to review your first professional index as my gift to you. Hopefully having me in the background to review your work and make suggestions will, somewhat, ease the dread of turning in that first professional index. A friend of mine, when he was faced with sending in his first professional index, found that he just could *not* hit that Send (Enter) button, and his wife had to step up to the keyboard and press it for him! Please try to give me a few days' notice (as you know from our association during this class just how frenzied my life normally is).

Remember: The Universe Rewards Action

I see great things on the horizon for you in this career field. You have great potential and I believe that you will make a successful and extremely competent indexer. You need to believe in yourself also! Trust that you came to this place for a purpose and follow your heart and your instincts in all that you do. This is the end of our student-teacher relationship and the beginning of a long-term colleague-colleague relationship. Please stay in touch … and remember that the weekly evening chat sessions are open to UCB graduates also. It's a wonderful and simple way to keep up to date on what's what, and the chats provide an easy way for you to get your burning questions answered. Get started today and take a step every day to get to where you want to go. Remember, the universe rewards action!

Contributors

Connie Binder has been a freelance indexer since 1999. With degrees in anthropology and library science, Connie's first job out of library school was analyzing scientific grants for a database and cataloging research reports. When her boss took over the company's indexing division, she insisted that Connie learn to index, and a new career was born. A generalist, Connie is happy to index almost anything that comes her way, but history books and biographies are her favorites. She is a member of the American Society for Indexing (ASI) and has served on the board of directors, as a chapter officer, and as manager of the Sports-Fitness Indexing Special Interest Group. Certified by the Institute of Certified Indexers, Connie is dedicated to providing quality indexes and to promoting consistency and quality within the profession.

Glenda Browne is a freelance indexer of books, websites, and databases, and is also a librarian and a teacher of indexing. She has written (or co-written with Jon Jermey) three books on indexing: *Website Indexing* (Auslib Press 2004), *The Indexing Companion* (Cambridge University Press 2007), and *The Indexing Companion Workbook: Book Indexing* (self-published). Glenda is the representative for the Australian and New Zealand Society of Indexers (ANZSI) on the IDPF EPUB Indexes Working Group. Two of her indexes have been Highly Recommended in the ANZSI Medal Award, and, in 2007, she was awarded the IgNobel Prize for Literature for an article on alphabetizing index entries that start with "The." Glenda has been involved with AusSI/ANZSI since she became an indexer in 1988 and has filled various executive roles in the National (now Council) and NSW committees as well as serving as chair of the Education Committee Working Party, conference administrator, and newsletter editor. She is a long-term member of the ASI Web Indexing SIG. Glenda can be contacted at glendabrowne@gmail.com, or through her website at www.webindexing.biz or her Facebook page at tiny.cc/IndCompFB.

Eve Morey Christiansen began indexing in 2010. She completed the indexing course through the University of California–Berkeley and Enid L. Zafran's

Indexing Boot Camp. After discovering an especially welcoming community within ASI, she was excited to become further involved by becoming the co-chair of the Upper Midwest Chapter. With a BA in anthropology and international studies, experience from living in Central America, and fluency in Spanish, she specializes in indexing cultural studies books, but enjoys general interest topics as well, especially agricultural and gardening books. She currently resides in Iowa.

Mary Coe has been a freelance book indexer for 20 years, working in a wide range of subject areas. She has extensive database indexing experience, including the National Library of Medicine's MEDLINE database and the National Security Archive in Washington, D.C. She is currently a student in the Master of Information Studies course at Charles Sturt University and serves as the secretary of the New South Wales Branch of the Australian and New Zealand Society of Indexers. Mary lives and works in Sydney, Australia. She can be contacted at coe.mary@gmail.com or through her website at www.bookindexing.com.au.

Anne-Marie Downey has been an indexer for 15 years, specializing in medical and science indexing. She is based in Ohio and works with Columbia Indexing Group. Anne-Marie is a graduate of the University of North Carolina at Chapel Hill and holds degrees in journalism and political science. She spent her early career writing and editing for newspapers in the South and Midwest. She developed her medical and science specialty over years of indexing texts on such topics as the neuroscience of vision, hospital pharmacy practices, the genetics of monocots, molecular biology, environmental geology, and chemistry.

Linda S. Dunn has been a periodical indexer for over 30 years. Before becoming a freelance indexer, she was an editor and indexer for the *Film Literature Index*. Several times a year she teaches an online workshop, Periodical/Database Indexing, through the Continuing Education program of the Simmons Graduate School of Information and Library Science. Presentations include "The Unbearable 'Aboutness' of Periodical Indexing," "Everything Is Illuminated: The Mysteries of Controlled Vocabularies Explained," and "Going Global: Working in a Multilingual and Multicultural World," a panel discussion at the ASI 2011 conference in Providence, Rhode Island. Publications include the article "Names in the Performing Arts" in *Indexing Names*, and "Ten Things I Learned Teaching a Workshop on Periodical/Database Indexing Online" in *Key Words* (July–Sept. 2011).

Lucie Haskins lives in Woodland Park, Colorado, and became an indexer in 2000, after a long career in corporate America, with roles spanning the computer industry and management consulting. She specializes in embedded indexing and in computer- and business-related topics. She has served on the ASI board, on the ASI webmasters team, and in various officer positions, including chairperson, for the Rocky Mountain chapter. She has a BS degree in technical management and an MBA. Lucie loves to share her passion for indexing by talking about it to anyone who will listen! To that end, she has given workshops on embedded indexing to ASI chapters, at ASI national conferences, and to local university-level technical writing classes, and has instructed students enrolled in UC Berkeley's online indexing course.

Chuck Knapp is a taxonomy and indexing manager at Bloomberg BNA. He leads the Bloomberg BNA taxonomy team and has been in the Bloomberg BNA indexing department in metropolitan Washington, D.C. for 20 years. He oversees publication of indexes and finding aids for print and electronic products from its Legal Publishing Group as well as its Tax & Accounting Group. He works with a broad range of legal subjects ranging from bankruptcy to intellectual property law. Previously, he was the indexer for *U.S. Law Week* and *Supreme Court Today*, and he created the index for BNA's *Health Law & Business Series* that won the American Association of Law Libraries' 1997 Best New Product award. He authored the chapter on indexing court cases for the book, *Indexing Specialties: Law*. Chuck is a graduate of the University of Oklahoma School of Law, and he grew up in Kansas and Texas.

Lai Heung Lam was born and raised in Hong Kong. Lai worked in graphic design, translation, and marketing prior to immigrating to New Zealand. Having worked for many years in multinational companies in liaison roles, Lai enjoys the challenges of helping to bridge the cultural gaps between the East and West. Lai holds a BA in Japanese as well as a master's degree in library and information science. She came to indexing with a one-year project indexing the *New Zealand Chinese Journals Database* for the Auckland City Libraries. Lai currently works at the University of Auckland Library cataloging both English and Chinese resources.

Cynthia Landeen opened In.dex.trous for business in 1998, after reading an article in the Portland *Oregonian* about people who made their living from books, but didn't write them. One of the people interviewed for the article was an indexer. Cynthia was a consulting engineer before she began indexing. This job required knowledge of all levels of math, making her familiar with the language. She began indexing math when asked if she could repair an index. Although she is a generalist indexer who indexes everything outside of cookbooks, legal, Western medicine, or straight philosophy, she still gets calls from publishers that begin with "I understand you know math." Cynthia says she is honored to have been asked to write an article, believing that indexers are smart, dedicated to their craft, and interested in increasing their skills base.

Fred Leise has indexed on a freelance basis since 1995, specializing in scholarly works in the humanities, including East Asian history and civilization, international relations, and politics. Since 2000, he has also worked as a taxonomy and information architecture consultant for such clients as Abbott Laboratories, HP, Dow Corning, Disney, and Accenture. Most recently, he was manager of the taxonomy team at Sears Holdings Corporation. Fred has written and spoken extensively on controlled vocabularies and indexing, presenting workshops at the annual conferences and regional meetings of ASI, the Information Architecture Institute, and the Special Libraries Association. He has taught indexing for the University of Chicago Publishing Program and the Graduate School of Library and Information Science of Dominican University (River Forest, IL). Fred has served several terms on the national board of ASI, including one term as president. He is a founding member of the Institute of Certified Indexers.

Frances S. Lennie is the owner of Indexing Research whose best-known product is CINDEX indexing software. She graduated from the University of Hull (U.K.) with honors in geography and economics, acquired graduate certificates in education and computer science, and worked as a teacher and National Institutes of Health research project coordinator before embarking upon her indexing career in 1977. Initially specializing in clinical and research medical texts, she now indexes in a variety of subject areas but especially education texts. From 2001 to 2006, she taught the semester-long "Indexing Books" unit for NYU's School of Continuing and Professional Studies Certificate in Editing course. Deeply committed to the purpose and goals of ASI, she has served as treasurer and president, and is extremely proud of two initiatives—the ASI Training Course and the Digital Trends Task Force (DTTF)—that she was able to facilitate, encourage, and support while under her watch. She has served as a juror for the Wilson Award, and, in 2005, she was honored to receive the Hines Award for her continuous and dedicated service to ASI. Frances lives in Rochester, New York, with her husband.

Celeste Newbrough, principal indexer of Academic Indexing Service (AIS), has over 20 years of experience as a classification specialist in natural sciences, social sciences, humanities, and international studies. Retired from the University of California–Berkeley, Celeste taught at City College of San Francisco and the Harvey Milk Institute, and served as Chief Information Officer for Cubedex in Cambridge, Massachusetts. She holds an MA from San Francisco State University and a BA from Louisiana State University. AIS has composed indexes for major academic and institutional publishers including The Smithsonian Institute, The MIT Press, University of California Press, Harvard University Press, University of Minnesota Press, The World Bank, University of Hawaii Press, and others.

Scott Smiley has been an ASI member since 1999 and indexing full time since 2001. He indexes scholarly, professional, and trade books as well as textbooks, primarily in the social sciences, humanities, environmental studies, and related subjects. Scott is also an instructor for Basic Indexing through the Graduate School USA (formerly USDA). He has used CINDEX for Mac throughout his indexing career and has given several workshops and panel presentations at national and chapter ASI meetings on both CINDEX and the use of patterns.

Martin White has been an indexer since 1982. He worked in the indexing department of *Encyclopaedia Britannica* for 13 years. Martin has been a full-time freelance indexer since 1995. His clients are mainly university presses, but he does index the odd trade book and a few medical journals. Martin's index to John Patrick Diggins's *The Promise of Pragmatism* received the 1995 ASI–H.W. Wilson Award. He contributed the chapter on indexing biographies to *Index It Right! Advice from the Experts, Volume 1*, the chapter on indexing philosophy in *Indexing Specialties: Scholarly Books*, and the chapter on indexing biographies in *Indexing Names*.

Enid L. Zafran has been indexing since 1975, and her business, Indexing Partners LLC, specializes in legal, public policy, scholarly, art, education, history, and psychology topics. A past president of ASI, Enid has served ASI in many capacities as a board member and as chair of the publications committee. She writes extensively on indexing, contributing to many of ASI's books as well as writing a column entitled "Indexing A to Zafran" in *Key Words*, the ASI newsletter. In previous positions, Enid has managed in-house indexing departments and has taught indexing at the Catholic University School of Library Science. She holds both a JD and a Masters in Library Science. In 2011, Enid received the Hines Award from ASI in recognition of her contribution to the profession of indexing. She is a founding member of the Institute of Certified Indexers, the only certifying organization for indexers in the U.S.

Index

Eve Morey Christiansen

Tables are indicated by "t" following page numbers.